OUR CHILDREN, OUR FUTURE
Living Ethics with Children

Lesley R. Vann, M.Ed.

Endorsements

Our Children, Our Future, should be considered as a spiritual text for teachers as well as parents. Author Lesley Vann, M.Ed. provides us with a guidebook that beautifully presents spiritual, moral and ethical teachings in ways that will enhance the development of a child's character and self-esteem. This book is a treasure."
> – Caroline Myss, Author
> *Intimate Conversations with the Divine, Anatomy of the Spirit*, many more, Five-time New York Times bestselling author

This is a book of deep spirit. The mainstream educational system spends most of its attention and time preparing children for jobs but this book reminds parents and teachers of the paramount importance of preparing children for life – which means learning more than reading and writing, math and science. The book shows powerfully and convincingly how children can be taught the art of relationships, how they can cultivate the qualities of their hearts, how to evolve their consciousness and how to learn to love. Author Lesley Vann has performed a great service to teachers and parents by writing such a timely and profound book and by bringing attention to these vital aspects of our children's education.
> – Satish Kumar, Editor Emeritus, *Resurgence & Ecologist*

All of us can make a difference in the world by practicing and living our highest values. Lesley Vann has given us guidelines for how to reflect on and develop these values in our homes and schools—providing our children with values to sustain them throughout life. Nothing can be more important than transforming our material values into the loving values that will create a new world—starting with our children.
> – Nancy Roof, Ph.D., Co-Founder of The Values Caucus, UN, Founder, *Kosmos Journal*

Lesley Vann's new book is a formidable and thoroughly documented recognition of the need for education to focus on values and ethics. Author Vann reminds parents and teachers that the inner life of a child most often forecasts whom each child will become in their personal future. She informs us how these values and ethics encompass learning to value all of life. Each value and ethic are explored deeply leading to a fuller understanding and practical outcomes. Recognizing children as the designers of the future, author Vann develops a wonderful educational model so that our children can experience and embody compassion and equity for all. As we educate for values and ethics, we are building an 'Authentic Education' as the hallmark for fostering a truly loving world—living as one humanity in a culture of peace and sustainability.

> – Nina Meyerhof, Ed.D
> Founder of Children of the Earth and One Humanity Institute Co-author, *Conscious Education*: The Bridge to Freedom Recipient: The Mother Theresa Award, Citizens Department of Peace Award, The International Educators Award

In *Our Children, Our Future*, Lesley Vann, M.Ed reveals deep wisdom and understanding of the Higher Values and Ethics every person must learn to embody to make a better life. Her book is a gift for all ages and audiences, especially parents, teachers, and young adults beginning their life's journey. Vann thoroughly discusses and teaches us how to facilitate and foster these necessary values and ideals within our children and ourselves so we may become healthy and successful citizens in our families, communities, and the world. *Our Children, Our Future* is pertinent to the familial and societal challenges we face today; it should be a life primer.

> – Sherla A. Evans, M.A., Educator, Southfield Public Schools, Michigan Oakland County, Michigan

Lesley Vann has provided the reader with both timely and timeless wisdom to both parents and teachers. How we educate children is how we elevate our societies, our cultures, and our world. To transform the souls of children we transform our collective future. It is though transmission of core values and ethics that we facilitate true alignment now and in the future.

> – Dr. Michael A. Glick, Psychologist, Dallas, TX

© 2025 by Lesley R. Vann

First Printing 2025

All rights reserved. No part of this publication may be reproduced or transmitted in any form or by any means, graphic, electronic or mechanical, including photocopying, recording, taping or information storage and retrieval systems, without written permission from the author.

ISBN 978-1-7341800-5-3

 *Veronica Lane Books*

Books That Make a Difference!

11420 US-1, N. Palm Beach, FL USA
Tel: +1(833) VLBOOKS +1(833-852-6657)

www.veronicalanebooks.com
email: etan@veronicalanebooks.com

All quotes taken from the works of Torkom Saraydarian are used with the permission of The Creative Trust.

Library of Congress Cataloging-In-Publication Data
Our Children, Our Future / by Lesley R. Vann
    - 1st Edition
    p. cm.

OUR CHILDREN, OUR FUTURE

Living Ethics with Children

Lesley R. Vann, M.Ed.

 Veronica Lane Books

Dedication

To parents everywhere, who hold the future in their families and in their hearts. To parents, teachers, grandparents, and caregivers everywhere, who hold the beauty, future, and purpose of children's potential in their hands. To all of us who envision the highest and best for the human family. May our lives and our planet be blessed with peace, beauty, and the highest unfoldment of potential that the world and history have ever seen. *We hold it in our hands, in our hearts, in our creative imaginations, and in our future thinking, to make this vivid dream a concrete reality.* May children and families everywhere be blessed on the wings of truth and Godspeed. Our children are our future, and we are invited to explore living ethics and virtues with our children, for they will further craft a world of safety, purpose and pioneering achievements, leaving a lasting legacy for the benefit of all.

Acknowledgments

Torkom Saraydarian (1917–1997) was an Armenian-American musician and author. His works represent a synthesis of the sacred culture of the world by creating a truly universal approach to spirituality. Torkom taught for over 50 years in the US and internationally, and counseled thousands of people. His written legacy spans over 170 books plus hundreds of musical pieces and lectures. I quote a lot from the works of Torkom Saraydarian because his teachings apply beautifully to all the important principles we discuss in this book.

Maria Montessori (1870-1952) was an Italian physician, educator, and innovator, acclaimed for her unique educational philosophy and methods that build on the way children learn naturally. She opened and ran the first Montessori school—the Casa Dei Bambini (Children's House)—in the slums of Rome beginning in 1907. Subsequently, she traveled the world, taught, and wrote extensively about her approach to education, attracting many educators and supporters. There are now thousands of Montessori schools in countries worldwide.

For many years, I was the director of early childhood and elementary Schools. I believe Dr. Montessori's writings are invaluable to any educator and parent, whether her method or school programs are accessed or not. Her philosophy and understanding of childhood and "discovering the child" can strengthen any school and family. One does not need to be a supporter or proponent of Montessori education to benefit from this book. It is noteworthy as well, that Jean Piaget was also a student of Maria Montessori. There are many wonderful approaches to education. I hope the reader will enjoy those quotes of Dr. Montessori that are offered here.

Introduction

Dear Reader,

Welcome! *Our Children, Our Future: Living Ethics with Children* is offered as a guide for parents and teachers. It is designed to be a living workbook to evoke thoughts and aspirations on your journey to excellence in parenthood and education. If you are a parent or a teacher, you already know that we all share the responsibility for molding our children's futures. The goal of this book is to be of support to you in this wonderful endeavor.

Perhaps it would be useful to sketch the background or context for this book. It came about during my tenure at Omega Vector, a volunteer seminar organization project headquartered in Phoenix, Arizona, U.S.A. Omega had sprung from the *Human Potential Movement* inspired by the writings of Teilhard de Chardin, as a self-mastery seminar to present concepts of unconditional love and sacrificial service. It was provided by a Phoenix couple who wanted to "give something back to humanity." The seminar was offered free to all and presented by a team of volunteer professional facilitators and psychologists.

It was the founders' dream to launch an *Omega School* – a school of the future, which would combine state-of-the-art in education, brain research, and brain-compatible education while promoting the tenets of love and sacrificial service for one humanity. I was asked to work on this project. As I considered the Omega landscape, it occurred to me that the most vital ingredient of the school had yet to be conceived; that is, an arsenal of trained teachers whose hearts and minds would be alive with this shared vision, and who would abide in lives of discipline and *Living Ethics.* Assuming their enthusiasm for a school of this kind, their hearts and minds still had to be cultivated and integrated before a school could be opened.

The Greek *ēthikē is defined as* the science of morals, based also on the Greek *ēthos*, meaning moral character or disposition. If we define *Living Ethics* as a path by which we can be very present today in our study of positive and enduring individual and societal morals (defined from the Latin *moralis* as customs or norms), then *Our Children, Our Future* is an attempt to develop a path for conscious teachers and aspiring parents. The book can be used on its own, perhaps even as a manual or as part of a training program and offered to parents and teachers via wider dissemination. While the book is written with this constituency in mind, it also tries to serve a broader audience; that is, any interested parent, grandparent, teacher, child-life professional, or caretaker of a child who is willing to consider the child, family, school and society in a new and expanded light. With this perspective, readers can seek to model virtues in their lives—to *live* ethics with and for the children in their lives.

To this end, the book seeks to inspire and motivate the reader to become the best role model/teacher/parent possible. It provides specific chapters on values and virtues to cultivate hearts and minds. The reader is invited to assist the child in becoming integrated and whole, to sidestep the modern concern with approval-seeking outside oneself, and to develop the child's infinite capacities! You are invited on an adventure of living ethics with your children, as a bridge to all children's futures. Our children will hold the reins and inherit the responsibility to create a safe and peaceful world. Living ethics can help them build that bridge to serve on behalf of all humanity.

– Lesley R. Vann

Table of Contents

Endorsements	ii
Dedication	vi
Acknowledgments	viii
Introduction	x
Educating the Heart	1
The Values	3
Love	5
Compassion	16
Acceptance	28
Responsibility	40
Integrity	50
Contentment	54
Courage	58
Giving	63
Tenderness	68
Patience	71
Trust	79
Persistence and Perseverance	83
Humility	87
Harmlessness	94
Forgiveness	98
Respect	108
Joy	113
Sincerity	127
Discipline	129
Simplicity	131
Diligence	134
Beauty	137
Culture	143
Adaptability	149
Closing Notes	153
References and Bibliography	156

Chapter 1
Educating the Heart

One can never step higher than himself with his mind, but every step onward of the heart carries you toward light. The mind gives you theories, advice, knowledge - but the heart shows you the way of transformation.
— Torkom Saraydarian
Challenge for Discipleship, p. 260.

The heart is called a chalice...the heart is called the guiding light of life.
— Torkom Saraydarian
The Heart and Its Twelve Petals

These values affect the education of the world. Those who respond to these values are creating a new educational system that will lead the world into the world of values and guarantee its survival and creative expressions.
— Torkom Saraydarian
The Psyche and Psychism, p. 891

There is an ancient legend from the East describing the 12 *Petaled Lotus of the Heart.* The petals it describes are humility, service, patience, love, group love, tolerance, self-forgetfulness, compassion, sympathy, wisdom, sacrifice, and gratitude. Whether this legend can be verified or not, we all know the qualities of a loving heart when we see them. We know the qualities or the spirit of brotherhood when we find it. The Platonists also wrote about the *12 Petaled Lotus of the Heart* and described these petals as virtues. The discussion of virtues has been with us since human societies were first formed in the early millennia of human history. In this book, we deal with virtues through role modeling, the study of values and ideals, and education. The Latin *virtus* was derived from the root of man (*vir*) and came to mean valor, merit, and moral excellence. Value also derives from the Latin *valere* meaning worth. So, we can define virtues as having great worth, and certainly, the merit of these studies should be evident to anyone interested in human flourishing. Appreciation of the virtues and understanding them as societal values can be enhanced through education. There are inspiring fields of study called values clarification and values education. To cultivate our young people into responsible and humanitarian citizens who can and will contribute to humanity, it is vital that we educate both the heart and the mind, that we educate the heart of the child, as well as their intellect, and that we unite values, ethics, and humanitarian concerns into our homes and schools.

The benefits of the application of values in daily life also help the entire family and our society. Schools and communities begin to reflect values as they are assimilated by our children. Eventually, the face of our planet becomes changed as well. What an incredible power we are holding in our hands!

Chapter 2
The Values

> Values are those *magnetic visions* which challenge human beings to climb toward a life more abundant, on higher and higher planes, in ever-expanding relationships…
>
> Values are standards of achievements. Values are steps leading to enlightenment, joy, prosperity, freedom, and unity.
>
> The right attitude to values creates progressive changes in the seven departments of human endeavor: politics, education, philosophy and communication, art, science, religion, economics, and finance. Wrong response to values increases the suffering of the world. Values are pro-survival factors… They bring us success and victory.
>
> As individuals change their lives through the power of values, nations will change; humanity will change; and the transformation of the planet will be a fulfilled fact.
>
> – Torkom Saraydarian
> *The Psyche and Psychism,* pp. 890-1; 894

We can say that a civilization is built upon its values. Our daily lives reflect our values. In shaping human character, we come to see that quality education cannot exist without inculcating values. A thriving, productive family life is lived with the demonstration of positive and progressive values. Whether children are taught values directly or indirectly, they learn them. Mostly, they learn them through the example of adults but also, of course, from their peers. Far more than with our words, we teach children with our behavior and example. Ageless values and virtues, practiced with mindfulness serve purposefully in offering vital support to children and families.

Today, most parents and educators are searching and researching for ways to develop healthy and happy children. The need for guidelines and techniques for raising healthy children via the cultivation of virtues becomes a necessity. The guidelines we offer will enable us to raise creative and productive citizens who eventually also find fulfillment as parents and teachers themselves.

What then is the first step? We adults are the ones who must apply these values and virtues to our children's lives and must do so as well in our own lives. Our behaviors can and must be congruent with our highest aspirations and visions. When we live our values, we enable our inner beliefs to match our outer behaviors. It is we who will demonstrate a life of integrity, giving, and love in action. Our children will then experience these aspirations naturally. It is only through the example of the adults around our children that they will be able to live the high values we espouse and teach to them. Our shared humanity, complete with our weaknesses and foibles, calls us to a life of vision, virtue, and principle. This then becomes the domain of *Living Ethics*.

We are compelled to design and support the improvement of our individual, family, and school lives into welcomed transformation. Through our efforts to learn, live, and teach the values that lead to a life of *Living Ethics*, we can ensure a radiant future for ourselves and for the children we love and serve. Our children will inherit what we give them. Our children become the legacy of our highest heartfelt aspirations. These values, upon which we continue to improve, strengthen, and uplift our human lives. Eventually, we view our efforts as merely a continuum of the enhancement of human values derived from the very beginning of time!

Chapter 3
Love

The supreme duty of every creature is to love.

The greatest way to increase love is through the labor of responsibility which results in sacrificial acts.

Those who live in the light of beauty, joy, love, and freedom, live in the future and create a culture which will evoke the best creative powers from coming generations.

– Torkom Saraydarian
The Flame of Beauty, Culture, Love, Joy

The measure of understanding is the degree of love. One can memorize lines word by word, yet one remains dead if the knowledge has not been warmed by love.

Truly, when one learns to discern the emanations of feeling in others, one will perceive that precisely love above all attracts the Fire of Space. He who said, "Love one another," was a true Yogi. Therefore, we welcome each outburst of love and self-sacrifice. Just as a lever sets the wheels in motion, so does love inspire powerful responses... for love is the true reality and treasure.

– *Agni Yoga, 424*

Our Ability to Love

Love alone is capable of uniting living beings in such a way as to complete and fulfill them. For it alone takes them and joins them by what is deepest in themselves. All we need is to imagine our ability to love developing until it embraces the totality of men and the earth.

– Pierre Teilhard de Chardin
The Phenomenon of Man

Love is what all children need. Love is what all people need. If you think about it, love is what makes all of life possible. Love is what initiates life. Love is what brings life into being. Love is what nourishes life. Love is what sustains life. And the lack of love is what destroys life. It is the lack of love that is currently threatening our safety on the planet The old axiom, "Love makes the world go 'round" keeps proving its truth.

It is up to us to demonstrate love in our child's life. If we do that, we will guarantee the child the strongest foundation possible. Love will melt all barriers in their personal life. Love will work wonders later, in their professional life. Love will prove to the child what counts. Love will magnify the child's natural radiance. We are all learning how to love more. This is our great task. Just because we are not experts at loving does not mean we can't make the effort. We can succeed. We have all reached certain levels so far! In that, we are successful. We can require of ourselves to do better. We can think of every day as an opportunity to love more. To do more. To create more. To give more. We can work to become examples of love. We can ask of ourselves to learn this lifelong art of loving.

Even if we fall short of our high ideals, we can still respect our efforts. Instead of degrading ourselves, we can respect where we stand now. We can strive toward the light. We can work to surpass ourselves. We can aim to love more than we loved yesterday. In all of our efforts, our children will gain. In our sincerity, the child will grow. In our striving will be the results. In our life of example, the child will be inspired.

We can do something. We can make a difference in our child's life. We can demonstrate to the child a life of love and peace and beauty. We simply need the right goals, or a roadmap, and to make the efforts required. All we need to do is to keep going, to persevere and to not give up. Ever!

To love is a lifelong assignment. It is even our assignment from Life! Since we have a child in our care, Life has demanded of us that we become good at loving. We have the task of refining our skills so that eventually we will become experts. There is an old saying, "The expert is always the person from out of town."

Well, in the case of children, we cannot afford for that to be true! Our children's lives rest on our expertise. So does their future, and their destiny.

Learning to Love

The child can only learn what the child is shown. The child can only live what the child learns. This is a pep talk to remind us all of the intense value of love; and even more than the value, the very necessity of love. We must love, to survive. We must learn to love, to create the kind of civilization we want. A safe and prosperous life is our heritage. Love is one of its primary building blocks.

It is impossible to separate our personal goals from our goals for our civilization. Our individual goals for a good life are the same goals for our successful group life. Everyone wants freedom, love, and joy. This all sounds large and idealistic. True, it is. You might ask what this has to do with children. Well, we're talking about a good life for all—on a big scale! Yet without virtues, a person cannot even have a good life. When we magnify the significance, we find that seven thousand or seven billion people are all individuals, too.

Each person on the planet is just one person multiplied. Each one is important. And we are part of a large human family. So is each of our children. Once a child really learns their individuality, their whole life will upgrade. Their behavior will become congruent with the highest and most beautiful aspects within the child. It has been said that love is humanity's goal. And that is our mission. Love is our goal as we reach toward (what Teilhard de Chardin called), "the Omega Point," the highest ideals we espouse for ourselves and our children.

Love is emphasized in the curriculum of most Montessori schools. The child's teachers are educated in the ways of love, freedom, and respect. A school that will really serve children must be founded on love. It must be founded on values that are life-enhancing. That will be the child's ticket to the future. For love is the keynote of brotherhood.

Love at Home and School

The child must be nurtured at both home and school. The child must be loved in both places. School is not meant to be a sterile place, a dry or empty place. School must be a place of love. The child must learn the message that the child is loved, that the child is good, and that the child is OK. That cannot happen in the sterility of old-style classrooms.

When schools become outmoded, change is necessary. Schools are changing. People's attitudes are changing. Love and tenderness are now accepted. Science is revealing the connection between touch and health. Between love and better health. Between positive thinking and greater immunity from disease. Research is even revealing that our blood cells change after we think about love, kindness, joy, etc. Our thoughts, words, and actions are key to our good health. Everything works together in concert.

Thank goodness many schools now encourage teachers to show love and respect. In Montessori schools, for example, teachers work in teams in each classroom and have the opportunity to put several minds to work for their children and families. Children have the chance to experience how several adults may work together in harmony and mutual respect with shared goals and visions for the children, for education, and life. What an opportunity for all! The following is an excerpt from Maria Montessori on the subject of love.

The Child's Love for Life

It is love that enables a child to observe keenly and ardently those features of their environment which are quite insignificant to adults because they lack a child's animation. Does not love make children sensitive to things which are noticed by everyone? Does not love reveal to children details and special qualities that are not appreciated by onlookers? Because the child is in love with their environment and not indifferent to it, a child's intelligence can see what is invisible to adults.

A child's love of their surroundings appears to adults as the child's natural joy and vivacity of youth. But the child does not necessarily recognize it as a spiritual energy, a moral beauty that accompanies creation.

A child's love is by nature simple. The child loves so that he may receive impressions which that are growth-producing. This is a natural and dynamic feature of child development.

The special object of a child's affection is the adult. The child receives from the adult the material help the child needs and earnestly asks for as part of the child's requirements for their self-development. For the child, the adult is a kind of venerable being. From their lips, as from a spring, the child draws the words they must learn to speak.

We should remember that a child loves us and wants to obey. A child loves an adult beyond everything else, and yet the reverse is usually heard: 'How those parents love their child!' or 'How those teachers love their pupils!' Further, it is said that children must be taught to love their mother and father, their teachers and fellow men, and even plants and animals.

But who teaches the child all that? Who can teach one how to love? Will it be the adult who calls out all of their childish manifestations or tantrums, and who only thinks of defending their possessions from the child? An immature adult cannot be a teacher of love. A caring adult can model that crucial sensitivity that we now call 'emotional intelligence.' Children learn from their role models and can develop their emotional intelligence through positive adult interactions.

Yes, the love of a child is of utmost importance. Fathers and mothers may not see everything, and they need a new being to rouse and to re-animate themselves with a fresh and living energy that they may no longer possess. The child needs a being who acts differently and who can say to the child each morning: 'Rise to and live the life! Learn to live better!' Yes! To live better! To feel the breath of love!' Without children to assist us, men would degenerate. If an adult does not strive to renew the self, a hard crust begins to form around them which will eventually make them insensitive.

– Maria Montessori
The Secret of Childhood, pp.103-106

What strong words Montessori writes. When it comes to raising a child and impacting their young life, we cannot afford to mess around! We hold the key to the child's entire future. We must fulfill our duty to our children and life.

Loving by a Life of Example

Children absorb everything in their environments. The child is begging to learn and to know. The child is seeking to become all that the child can be. We can show the child the way through life by example, through a life of love, and through living the example of love. It takes our firm commitment, and recommitment. We commit and recommit to teach the child the lifelong art of loving. We can be inspired by what some visionaries have written about love. Let's think of ways in which you can learn and demonstrate more love in your life and at home. Journal and discuss as appropriate.

Another dimension of love expresses itself as a striving for the unity of mankind. At that stage, the person stands for total unity, and lives a unifying life. As we are living in a challenging period when more and more information is coming at us, particularly regarding national and international conflicts, people become more separated in their thinking and attitudes out of fear, survival, and protection instincts. We want to encourage people to learn not just tolerance but acceptance, and eventually even towards the child's goal of universal love.

More about Love

This list includes some qualities of love for us to contemplate and put into action:

- Love must be progressively expanding, inclusive, and creative.
- The child's nature of love is sacrificial.
- Love is the midwife of beauty.
- Love's nature is unconditional.
- Responsibility is one of the laws of the science of love.
- Love is unified, not separated.
- Love means to love everything in creation.
- Joy is a characteristic of love.
- Gratitude is a characteristic of love.

– Torkom Saraydarian
The Flame of Beauty, Culture, Love, Joy,
p. 133

Our inspiration for creative works, or sacrificial actions is nothing else but a downpouring of love. As deep as man goes into the energy of love, proportionately he becomes more creative and more radiant. (*Ibid.* p.152)

Ways of Loving

How do all these words about love affect us? Love affects our lives in every aspect. It affects our children. When we are committed to loving our lives will change. And so will our children. It is in an environment of love that the child will bloom. When does a child bloom?

- When you are an understanding person.
- When you give the child acceptance.
- When you accept the child for who the child is in the moment, and in the future.

- When you accept the child not by who you think the child should be.
- When you express love for your child in all conditions despite all conditions.
- When you are tolerant toward the child and not a fanatic about rules.
- When you exercise flexibility and openness.
- When you respond to each expression of the child according to the *spirit* of the ground rules, and *not the letter* of the ground rules.
- When your flexibility provides for the child the spirit of rules and does not always enforce the letter of the rules.
- When you are both consistent and yet flexible.
- When children know their limits and experience safety within those limits.

Demonstrating Love

By all our acts of acceptance, understanding, tolerance, and flexibility, the child will bloom. The child will grow and unfold. The child will show you their true spirit. The child will grow into love. The child will reflect maturity. The child can only live what the child has learned. What the child has absorbed, seen, and experienced. Give the child their due. Respond to the child with love and joy. Do your duty to the child and life. Love the child. Understand the child. Learn about the child. Accept the child without strings and conditions. Be flexible. Be joyful. When you have problems doing all that, then do some work on yourself: Work on your thoughts, words, feelings, and actions. Work on your attitudes. Keep in mind that your goal is to love the child unconditionally.

How? Decide to do that. Make the choice. Commit to love, again and again. Learn to love, again and again. Allow yourself to be a rookie in love, a learner. Tolerate your own mistakes and failures. Just pick up any messy pieces and go on. And never stop. Never. Remember, your child is depending on you to succeed. Your success will be their success, their strength, and their future. Your child is absorbing your essence. Strive to be as loving and caring as you possibly can. Start today, even if your child is not yet born!

Following is an inventory for you to reflect upon. Take some quiet time. Think about your skills, strengths, and weaknesses. As a person and a parent, everything is intertwined. Be honest. Be realistic. Be optimistic. Be hopeful. Tell yourself that even if you have never done that before, you *can* do it. You can become an expert at love and loving. Let's start now!

Inventory on Love

Ask yourself: When do I need to place more value on loving? How much? Ask yourself, how committed are you to loving? If you have resistance to loving unconditionally, think about it. Observe it. Do not judge yourself. Do not feel guilty about your resistance. Simply ask yourself what your resistance is. What is it saying to you? Do you want to learn from its message? Do you want to discover how to change your thoughts, feelings, and actions? What would you need to do differently to change? What new message can you give yourself to change? Ask yourself, "How can I best serve my child at this time?" You may journal on all these questions if you wish.

Then, picture yourself overcoming all your obstacles and becoming totally loving. See yourself filled with joy, beauty, love, and compassion. See yourself as patient. Feel joy within you as you see ideal pictures in your mind. See yourself happy, your children and family happy and radiant. Smile. Believe that it is so. Do this as many times as necessary until you feel small and great changes in your life until you feel the love your child needs for their future. You can become skilled at loving. You can become skilled at whatever you commit to entirely. Record your progress. Believe in yourself, and go forward. Trust yourself. Trust your child. Trust life! Radiate joy!

Chapter 4
Compassion

> Compassion sees in all imperfections the perfection, the future, and in all contradictions, the harmony. Compassion is the fountainhead of Love.
>
> – Torkom Saraydarian

Compassion is so important in a child's life. Children must not only learn to become compassionate as they reach maturity, but they must also be exposed to it in their environment. Since this world generally demonstrates non-compassionate behavior, caring adults must work overtime to demonstrate compassion to children.

This is a big project. Adults need to demonstrate compassion in their relationships with both children and other adults. They need to understand what makes people tick and arrive at a realistic yet hopeful portrait of human nature. They must come to terms with their own humanness and weaknesses in order to learn acceptance. From such acceptance comes love, patience, and the quality of non-criticism. This leads to non-judgment, non-condemnation. It is in this context that compassion is born.

Compassion is the only glue that can cement positive human relationships. When we do not demonstrate compassion, we create conflict, misunderstanding and problems. We nurture a distortion of thinking. We create boundaries and cleavages between people—within ourselves, and within families and communities.

The lack of compassion on the part of adults has sabotaged children throughout history. Now is the time for us to begin to undo this age-long damage. Only by children growing up in a compassionate environment will they become well-rounded, sensitive adults. To be prepared for fulfillment in life, every child must gain the basics of compassion. Otherwise, they will continue to alienate those they love and sabotage their own lives. To attain some measure of compassion, children must interact with compassionate adults since adults are the primary role models for children. Further, they must be exposed to compassionate environments as much as possible.

All of this is easier said than done. Yet, we must make sincere and persistent efforts to create compassion—within ourselves, our homes, schools, and families. We owe this not only to our children but to ourselves, to our families and to our communities. This obviously requires a shifting of attitudes, and these shifts will differ from person to person. Making the effort to cultivate the compassion already within us is the first step; next, we begin to demonstrate it in increasing amounts. This is a process, not an overnight phenomenon. Seeking to accomplish and actually accomplishing our goals requires many of our inner resources. We will be drawing upon our deepest selves, as well as our more superficial parts. It will involve both knowing, being and doing. Following are some notes on compassion and some activities for adults to use alone and with children.

Notes on Compassion

- Compassion involves selflessness.

- It involves the overcoming of our own petty lives, and our own egos for the uplifting of others, who are part of ourselves and the whole.
- With compassion, we can walk in the other person's shoes; we grow to feel the other person's needs, their hearts and their trials.
- When we are compassionate, we care and we are caring people.
- Compassion is the ability to act according to what you know another person really needs or really wants.
- Compassion links and unites; it builds bridges between people and creates harmony.
- Compassion creates trust between people or between groups.
- Compassion makes a person more sensitive to their environment.
- Compassion enables us to truly love another person, and not for our own needs.
- Compassion is the tool needed to create harmony within ourselves, our families, and our world.

Some Forms of Compassion

- Thinking of the needs of another person with a genuine concern.
- Sincerely caring about people by anticipating their needs and wants.
- Giving of ourselves to others.
- Outward expression of our energies; our concerns turn outward.
- Knowing our responsibilities.

- Active listening; that is, listening with ears, heart, and mind.
- Giving one's full attention to others.
- Looking and really seeing, listening, hearing, experiencing and really feeling another.
- Being filled with concern and striving to meet the needs life demands of us.
- Knowing what is happening in the world. Becoming aware of world events.
- Getting to know the people around us as much as possible so that we understand them better.
- Having a certain degree of detachment; that is, looking down at a situation from a higher level so that we may observe it. In observing it we are drawn towards compassion which derives from a greater understanding.
- Knowing as much history of a situation as possible so that we may empathize.
- Intuiting the needs of others based on the humanness we know within us.
- Knowing the hearts of others because we know our own hearts.
- Allowing fondness for others to develop.
- Allowing devotion and dedication to others.
- Seeing a universal cause or vision that uses and facilitates compassion.
- Having a reverence for others expressing itself through respect, thoughts, words, feelings, and actions.

Components of Compassion and Its Uses

- Kindness.
- Giving.
- Service rendered unconditionally.
- Spontaneous outflow of a loving heart and an enlightened mind.
- Wisdom.
- Serenity.
- Inner strength and being grounded.
- Feeling of personal autonomy that is strong enough to give to others.
- Heartfelt help to others.
- Sensitivity and awareness of the needs of others.
- Increased sense of responsibility.
- Humility and the ability to be taught by others.
- Willingness to be guided by the unfoldment of a relationship.
- Clear understanding of someone's life or dilemma.
- Giving someone the benefit of the doubt as appropriate.
- With children: Compassion can emerge from knowing that children will face challenges in the areas of discipline, through their interactions with others, learning what is appropriate behavior and what is not, learning about their bodies. Once we realize the sensitive plight of children, we more easily respond in service to them out of compassion.
- Life experience teaches us compassion.
- Trial and error promote compassion, as we realize the complexities within every situation.
- Our compassion enables a child to live life and discover life.

- Without our compassion, children lead hampered lives, stifled lives.
- Compassion can free children appropriately, whereas, non-compassion enslaves them.
- Compassion leads to greater freedom and greater self-actualization.
- Compassion dissolves the barriers between people; between parent and child, spouse and spouse, and ultimately in all relationships.
- Compassion recognizes the beauty within each person, despite behavior, habits, and distorted thinking.
- Compassion does what it can for the service of others and for a greater vision.
- Compassion bridges the hearts of people.
- Compassion creates understanding between people.
- Compassion inspires dedication and dedicated service.
- Compassion evokes sacrifice.
- In service to our children, the purpose of compassion is to give them a childhood and a life filled with support, love, and dedicated parenting—fulfilled with qualities they need in order to develop their physical, emotional, and mental selves. These qualities include cozy, inviting, child-adapted areas for home, school, work, and play.
- Compassion results in our own inner transformation.
- Compassion is the path to personal awareness and growth.
- Compassion grows levels of love within us.
- Compassion deepens commitment.
- Compassion requires that we know our own history of pain and suffering, and the experience we have gained from these.
- Setting a high value on compassion.

- Compassion enhances our abilities to more deeply empathize with others, to know how others are feeling, understanding and sympathizing with their experiences.
- Compassion increases a genuine concern for the well-being and rights of others.
- Compassion requires the sincere reaching outside of ourselves; with questions, discussions, concerns, statements, and interest about others and about their worlds.
- Compassion requires some personal sacrifice while expecting nothing in return.
- Compassion is the greatest character builder; the bigger hearts we have; the more love, joy, beauty and compassion we develop and express.

Activities for Cultivating Compassion

The personal, inner work of developing compassion is vitally important. Think about compassion and what it means to you. Consider your degree of compassion. Now, finding a quiet place to reflect and contemplate, try answering these questions:

- How skilled in its use are you?
- How committed to it are you? When are you compassionate and when not?
- What stops you from being compassionate?
- When are your blocks to compassion aroused?
- What quality or qualities do you need to overcome within you and in your life to be more compassionate?
- What would these changes entail?
- How much do you want to make these changes?
- What is stopping you?
- Who would benefit from your compassion?

- Who is losing out when you are not compassionate?
- Who loses when they experience your levels of non-compassion?
- Who is responsible for your behavior?

Discussions on Compassion:

- Discuss these points with people close to you or with your significant other.
- Think about these points and their application in your personal and family life.
- Write in your journal about these points.
- Read active listening books. Do active listening exercises. Practice active listening with children, family, and friends.
- Develop and refine your empathy skills.
- Form active listening techniques. (Suggested reading: Parent Effectiveness Training by Dr. Thomas Gordon and P.E.T. in Action by Dr. Thomas Gordon)
- Choose to be fully present, aware, caring, and receptive to the needs of others.
- Call local crisis intervention centers and hotlines, to ask for their tips on developing empathy.
- Request handouts and printed material on empathy training and skills.
- Develop greater gratitude i.e., count your blessings, plus love and appreciation in all aspects of your life.
- Enlarge your ability to be flexible. Practice greater flexibility in areas where you exhibit resistance, denial, avoidance, fear, or jealousy.

- Push yourself to expand, to reach outside yourself, to others and to find more creative solutions that stretch your previously defined limits.
- Find the ways in which you have been holding yourself and others back in life—acting as an obstacle. Make the inner commitment to overcome this dysfunctional behavior. See how it is outdated and how it is sabotaging your life and other's lives, noting how it is preventing you from experiencing real joy.
- Experiment and shift some of your outworn attitudes, habits and behavior. Feel the joy of giving to others, of working for their happiness and well-being.
- Charge yourself with goodwill.
- Realize there are many viewpoints and sides to a story, and that many of them are valid.
- Overcome the need to judge, compare, and to always be right.
- Let go of habits, thoughts, and patterns that are self-righteous. Recognize how and where your self-righteousness and vanity sabotage your relationships, as well as your ability to be truly successful and at peace in your life and work.
- Consider the link between your vanity and your lack of compassion.
- See how you may be ego-centered with your need to be right.
- See how being ego-centered along with your need to be right end up blocking your love flow and your reaching out to others. Recognize this as the work of the ego.

- Find ways that are appropriate for you to begin chiseling away at vanities and selfishness.
- Aim to develop greater compassion within your heart and feel confident that eventually your efforts will pay off.
- Do you see how our self-centered lives defy compassion but also provide the motivation to do our inner work?

All of the above can be used as discussion points, family themes for games and talks, and as content to expand upon in your journals and talks with friends. Make it a point to reach outside of yourself by asking questions, initiating discussions, making statements, expressing deep and sincere concern for others, as well as for events and conditions outside yourself and your family.

Consciously consider your role, possibly in the larger picture; that is; in the well-being of your community, society, and world at large. Ponder this larger picture and write about it in your journal if you are inspired. As we expand our considerations and viewpoints, as we become more broadminded and inclusive, we grow more compassionate.

Cultivating Compassion In Children

Speak often to your children about people and their needs. Talk with them about why people probably do what they do, or say what they say. Initiate discussion about people and what makes them tick. Help children learn to understand others and to realize that everyone has challenges, weaker qualities, and conflicts—that they are not the only ones to have a problem—and that the needs and wants of others are just as important as theirs; that other people have rights too and that these rights must be respected because they are important.

In watching television, movies, plays, and in reading stories with children, bring up for discussion questions about why the characters involved would have done what they did, felt what they felt, thought what they thought. This kind of family and school discussion may be among the most important in helping the child understand himself and other people; what makes us tick and in learning to really care about others. Further, from this kind of activity the child can over time learn to respect and accept themselves and human nature in general because the blessing of a deep understanding, and thus compassion, can be felt for all people.

Make a special time to answer children's questions about other people's responses to them individually, about their concerns in day-to-day life and some of the issues they face. Help the child dissolve the mysteries and some of the accompanying fears the child will develop in second guessing the behavior of others. Do all you can to help the child learn to give others the benefit of the doubt, and to learn to use real discernment in order to do their best as to what is appropriate in the appropriate condition.

Use and repeat often the theme of *caring* with your children; that is, caring for themselves, caring about others, caring about nature, plants and animals, caring about their friends and families, caring about people less fortunate, caring about people in other countries who are hungry, poor or sick.

Highlight your family discussions and talks with your children with this theme of caring. Do all you can to promote caring within your family and within your life in general. Make home and school caring environments. This means the prevailing feeling is that children are cared for and loved, that the adults are also cared for; and that everyone has the opportunity to express their love, affection, and care for others.

All these pointers also apply to relatives, neighbors, babysitters and family friends. This extends to animals, plants, and flowers, as well as to things in the environment which require care and respect, such as clothing, furniture, and books.

Help children become more broadminded and expanded in their viewpoints and considerations. Daily life and events are the best arena in which to build these skills. We can teach compassion to our children.

Chapter 5

Acceptance

> I accept myself completely here and now, and consciously experience everything I feel, think, say, and do, as a necessary step toward my growth into greater awareness.
>
> — Ken Keyes, Jr.,
> *Handbook to Higher Consciousness*

> I accept you as you are; as you have been in the past; and as you may become in the future.
>
> — Ed Clark,
> *Glad to Be Me: Building Self-Esteem in Yourself and Others*, Dov P. Elkins

Declaration of Acceptance and Owning (for reading aloud)

I accept and own me. In all the world there is no one else exactly like me. There are persons who have some parts like me, but no one adds up exactly like me. Therefore, everything that comes out of me is authentically mine because I alone choose it.

I accept and own everything about me—my body and everything it does; my mind—including all its thoughts and ideas; my eyes, including the images of all they behold; my feelings, whatever they may be: anger, joy, frustration, love, disappointment, excitement; my mouth, and all the words that come out of it: polite, sweet or rough, correct or incorrect; my voice, loud or soft; and all my actions, whether directed towards others or to myself.

I accept and own my fantasies, my dreams, my hopes, my fears. I accept and own all my triumphs and successes, all my failures and mistakes. Because I accept and own all of me, I become intimately acquainted with me. By so doing I can love me and be friendly with me in all my parts. I thereby make it possible for all of me to work in my best interests.

I accept and own the aspects about myself that puzzle me and the aspects that I do not know. Regardless, I remain friendly and loving to myself. I courageously and optimistically look for the solutions to these puzzles in order to find out more about me.

However I look and sound, whatever I say and do, and whatever I think and feel at a given moment in time comes from within me. This is authentic and represents where I am at that moment in time.

I accept and own how I looked and sounded in the past, what I said and did, how I thought and felt.

I accept and own that what transpired in the past may turn out to have been unfitting.

I accept and own that I can discard anything that is unfitting and keep that which has proved fitting, and invent something new for that which I discarded.

I accept and own all that I see, hear, feel, think, say and do.

I accept and own that I have the tools to survive any circumstance, to be close to others, to be productive.

I accept and own my intimacy with myself.

I accept and own my ability to be productive.

I accept and own my ability to creatively make order out of what appears chaotic, within myself and outside of myself.

I am Me and I am okay.

— Virginia Satir, *Glad To Be Me*

Acceptance

With acceptance, true acceptance, a child will grow into a wonderful adult. We all bloom in an atmosphere of loving acceptance. When we are accepting, we are open to life and to people. We can tolerate many conditions and events around us. We do not need to agree or submit to anyone else but we can experience a measure of freedom from criticism when we are accepting of others.

When a child lives with this kind of acceptance, the child grows strong and gains confidence. When we give children acceptance, we are acknowledging the beauty within them. We are making their words, thoughts, feelings and actions OK. We are giving them the message, both spoken and unspoken, that they are valuable.

When a person feels accepted, they feel loved, free to be themselves without pretense or deceit. A child who feels acceptance learns to trust. The child also is able to maintain those rare qualities of character that usually disappear in middle childhood--namely, faith, trust, love, and giving. What a magnificent culture we will create as our young citizens grow up retaining these magnificent character traits.

Some of the qualities we possess that are associated with acceptance:
- We are able to be on good terms with life.
- We are able to make things OK.
- We wait to judge, and do not pass judgment.
- We overcome our self-righteous opinions.
- We are open to life, to ourselves, and to others.
- We hold opinions but we do not force these on others.
- We allow others to develop and to be themselves.
- We give freedom and space to people and situations.
- We trust and we evoke trust from others.
- We sincerely demonstrate love and warmth.

- We have goodwill toward others.
- We are benevolent.
- We are magnanimous.
- We work for mutuality in life and conditions.
- We cultivate mutual respect in our relationships.
- We recognize other people's rights.
- We are committed to upholding others' rights.
- We acknowledge differences between us with joyousness and openness.
- We become inclusive in our thinking.
- We see the beauty in people and in their uniqueness.
- We understand a variety of opinions, habits and actions.
- We are tolerant and patient.
- We demonstrate forbearance.
- We feel filled with the spirit of goodwill.

Acceptance Includes:

- Developing trust in ourselves, others and life itself.
- Understanding humility and acting without arrogance.
- Loving with an open heart.
- Tolerating that which we feel may not be appropriate, as long as it is legal, moral and ethical.
- Allowing events, experiences, people, situations to play out in front of us.
- Finding the good and the potential beauty and joy in everything.
- Seeing or sensing the unity underlying all things; that is, the unity of life.
- Being open to life with a sense of the joy of discovery.
- Developing a universal interest in things.

- Avoiding harsh criticism.
- Giving validation and credence where due.
- Finding commonality.
- Working to create harmony in all things; among people, the family, and community.
- Understanding the sense and synthesis of all phenomenon.
- Empathy and seeing oneself in others.
- Not putting up barriers or walls.
- Putting aside undue fear of the events and conditions of life.
- Not compartmentalizing; seeing the whole.
- Avoiding undue stipulations, demands, expectations of others.
- Awareness; being very aware of what or who we reject.
- Being aware of intentional or unintentional shunning.
- Not a shying away nor denying challenging situations.
- Utilizing holistic thinking skills by opening to divergence of life.
- Initiating creativity wherever there is a call for it.
- Observing our habits of separation.
- Embracing our own moral path heartily as well as those of others.
- Making the changes we say we desire in ourselves.
- Doing the work that is ours to do toward our highest ideals.
- Finding peace for ourselves and others on the path of acceptance.

Accepting Self and Others

Accepting ourselves is necessary if we are going to accept others. We can only love others to the degree that we love and accept ourselves. This means that we accept and do not condemn every part of ourselves—the good, the beautiful, and the not-so good and not-so beautiful within ourselves. We validate ourselves and others, and we are careful in our judgments. We can always exercise choice once we have observed any person or situation.

We may come to see certain habits that we have as damaging to our health. Yet, we can acknowledge the fact that this habit must have served some purpose in our lives originally and that it has therefore had its place up until now. It has brought us this far. We may choose to drop smoking, drugs, or gambling and substitute new and better behaviors.

This way we do not condemn ourselves. We see what works in our lives and what sabotages us. We choose the path that we feel is most appropriate, allowing others to do the same. It has been said that all things are valid in their relative place in life. We do not need to join others on their path, but we can simply acknowledge the role they are serving in the progression of life. Ultimately, we can acknowledge and accept them in the same way we see a rattlesnake as a phenomenon of life. We can validate its existence. We just may not want to live with it! In the same way, we can validate tantrums and bedwetting in children. Even while disciplining them, we can express acceptance when our children behave in ways that we feel are inappropriate. We can clearly let them know their behavior is inappropriate, and at the same time, we let them know that they are wonderful people! When we do this consistently, children will receive the message that they count but that they may need to behave differently at home or school. This is one of the messages and gifts of acceptance.

Self-acceptance and our ability to accept others is directly connected to our level of self-esteem. To the degree that we trust and befriend ourselves, we are able to do so with others. Generally, the more we feel at the helm of our own lives (next to God, if this is your wish) the more autonomous and stronger we are in life, and the more enthusiastic and vital we are as whole individuals. People who are afraid to work toward what they truly want in life usually consider themselves victims of life. They feel helpless. They also do not trust themselves or others very much. They are afraid to move out of the safe territory beyond their daily grind.

Children want to discover life, to live life to its fullest, and to take various risks, thereby usually becoming skilled at trusting and loving themselves. This, in turn, allows them to become skilled at loving others.

What is self-acceptance all about? It is about our learning to drop the old beliefs which urge us to criticize and condemn. Self-acceptance is about becoming free from harsh or rash judgments and self-righteousness. It is about learning humility. It is about our becoming open to life. We do not consciously know all the answers. No one does. We are all learning. Yet, at some juncture in our lives, we must take the helm and decide we want to live a fulfilling life, within ourselves, within our family structures, society and in the world.

Self-acceptance calls for our resourcefulness and creativity! We are now on a new journey into the unknown. We must now venture to create newer attitudes which will allow us to be successful adults, parents and members of a global community. We must commit ourselves to drop the attitudes which have limited us, caused unnecessary self-criticism while condemning ourselves and others. In the jargon of modern psychology, this means that we are training ourselves to become more aware as we make immediate and oftentimes wrong judgements.

What are the characteristics of the accepting and more non-judgmental person? Following is an excellent appraisal of the actualized (or fulfilled) person as relates to self-acceptance by Lou Benson: "Another important area in which self-actualizing people differ from others is in their non-judgmental acceptance of themselves. Maslow says that these people seem to have a lack of overriding guilt and crippling shame and also to be free of the anxieties that usually accompany these feelings.

They can accept them. Owning human nature in the stoic style, with all its shortcomings and with all its discrepancies from the ideal is an image of feeling real concern but within the scope of comfort.

Such feelings of comfort and acceptance with the self are extremely important in terms of laying down a tone that underlies a person's whole existence. The difference between happiness and unhappiness is related to this tone.

The healthy individual does not strive to live up to an ideal, perfect PR image. They see themselves as human and therefore as unheroic in the naive sense. They acknowledge their so-called shortcomings, deficiencies and inconsistencies. In short, they acknowledge their imperfections without being disparaged by them.

Being accepting of their frailties, they can also be accepting of others' frailties. And the healthy person demands neither more nor less of others. They are willing to acknowledge human nature in all human beings, in others as well as in themselves.

One very important area in which self-actualizing people are accepting is on the animal level. They accept their animal nature without shame, without guilt, and with a kind of gusto or *joie de vivre*. They are lusty in their love of food, sex, and excitement, and they tend not to feel shame or disgust with the functions of the body on the animal level. Thus, they are less likely to respond negatively to these basic needs."

– Lou Benson
Glad to Be Me, Dov P. Elkins

Last Thoughts on Acceptance

Acceptance begins on the premise that we are OK. We are acceptable, all of us.

Our love and acceptance for others exists only in the proportion we have it for ourselves. We must possess acceptance to give it. How can we give what we do not have? And yet, our finding and claiming self-acceptance is a growing process, evolving and deepening as we mature. All of life is a maturing process. In the East, the weathered beauty of an aged face is considered the hallmark of wisdom. The aged are revered beyond compare. Maturity is sanctified through experience.

As we experience our own inner unfoldment and growth and our own expansion of consciousness, we express our wisdom to the world through all our creativity and maturity. We become centered and balanced people. We have equilibrium. From this type of foundation, we have joy and we learn to accept each other. We contribute to the welfare of those around us. We contribute to our children and their development. From this foundation we are the benefactors of life.

How can we translate all that we feel as acceptance into our everyday world of parenting, educating and loving? Simply by meeting each experience of life with an inner attitude of trust and awareness. Does this mean getting ourselves dirty?

Diapers, toilet-training, tantrums, shyness, bedwetting, anger, biting, all the traumas large and small, the not-so-nice side of childrearing is accepted. We see it all and we know that we must accept it all. As we move through the various processes, we become increasingly aware of our responses, both inner and outer and we see how we relay these to the very sensitive children we serve hour by hour. We remind ourselves while we are still integrating new behaviors to maintain our serenity, composure and calmness. If we find ourselves in an unusually challenging circumstance, we can choose with our willpower to stay calm and detached. As we gain more the role of the observer in conflicting situations, the situation no longer owns us. We do not react mechanically or habitually. We hold our own, stay centered, acting and not reacting, becoming ever more accepting.

Acceptance of life and its unfoldment will give us the key to contentment in our lives. There is the saying that all pain comes from resistance. Acceptance will override our former resistance and will set us free from the chains of false standards and pretenses, free from judgment, free from denial, free from avoidance, free from fear, and free from living defensively.

Acceptance means we will accept everything the child gives us and shows us. If it is against the ground rules, we have supportive techniques for home and classroom management. Acceptance of rule-breaking behavior does not mean we encourage it, nor praise or reinforce it. We simply do not insult the child or verbally abuse the child, embarrass them, or make them wrong. We take the appropriate adult and mature actions and then move on.

What an opportunity we as adults have to imbue the world's future leaders with the inner knowing that they are valuable, lovable, and capable, that they are accepted and respected! Acceptance begins on the premise that we are OK. We are acceptable, all of us.

Acceptance Activities

1. Consider some things you do not accept about your child, husband or wife.
2. Contemplate ways to accept and come to terms with these things.
3. Within yourself.
4. Within your relationship.
5. What behavior do *you* need to display in order to change those things?
6. Devise a plan to change them.
7. For one week, each day choose which disturbing behavior of your own or of others that you want to accept. You can silently and aloud say:

Today, I am open to accepting: _____

In addition to journaling, you can silently and aloud say this regarding your own personal traits, or of a family member, a neighbor, professional associates, or strangers.

As we work to resolve issues where acceptance is the key to finding holistic solutions, we find ourselves changing within and then noticing outward changes in situations and circumstances that arise in our daily lives. In finding acceptance within ourselves and acting more in accordance with acceptance, challenges seem to even resolve themselves. We become more effective as parents and provide a much healthier environment for our children.

> O, let the Self exalt itself,
> Not sink itself below;
> Self is the only friend of self,
> And self is Self's only foe.
> For self, when it subdues itself.
> It befriends itself.
> And so, when self eludes self-conquest, it remains its only foe.
> So calm, so self-subdued,
> The Self has an unshaken base,
> Through pain and pleasure, cold and heat,
> Through honor and disgrace.
> — Hindu Scriptures, 1st Century from *Glad to Be Me*, Dov P. Elkins

So much is a man worth as he esteems himself.
— Rabelais; *Ibid.* p. 37

The greatest evil that can befall a man is that he should come to think ill of himself.
— Goethe

Chapter 6
Responsibility

Responsibility is a key factor of a wholesome life. It is literally, the ability to respond to others and to ourselves. It derives from an action verb. Responsibility implies caring actions for ourselves, for others and for things. When we take responsibility, it means that we care, that we do the things which need to be done, we make changes, we oversee things, and we take action.

Responsibility initiates us into greater measures of self-reliance, independence, and accountability. A life lived responsibly creates harmony more than obstacles. When we live responsibly, we are harmless, meaning that we are not causing any grievances or conflicts. Responsibility is the flower of a life lived in accordance with our conscience, with our values, and our integrity.

Children are hungry for responsibility. They want to be given the recipe for living responsibly. They want to learn how to care for others, for themselves, and everything around them. Children want to assert themselves and thereby they start to learn about consequences. We want to teach them early on that thinking, speaking and acting in a responsible way will produce positive consequences and outcomes. This means that underneath their initial rebelliousness against learning responsibility, they actually do want to learn how to groom and care for their bodies, how to care for their clothes, toys, books, art materials, and how to keep their rooms neat and orderly.

Young children, especially before the difficult teen years, can be guided away from a social and media mindset that pushes self-gratification before caring for others. Particularly in wealthier societies, parents give up too easily on the task of teaching and enforcing responsibility, even with such simple requests as putting toys away neatly or simple etiquette. Sometimes, even when children are learning to be responsible, they are teased by peers for being too goody- goody. Grandparents out of sentiment sometimes prevent children from doing things for themselves in responsible ways, i.e., they may often pick up after their adorable little ones to avoid being stern, to be more lax than the parents in order to be more loved by their grandkids.

Taking care of ourselves, friends and loved ones, does not seem to be popular today. Responsibility is not "in." Rather, it is common to rely on others and even blame outside factors for the problems in our lives. Living with the utmost integrity and responsibility is demonstrated rarely in children's programming on television, radio, in books or video games. When responsibility is acknowledged, it is rarely portrayed in detail. In the lyrics of popular music, what it means to truly love another person is highlighted only in romantic terms, not in the reality that love equals responsibility. Children need to see adults speaking and acting responsibly in order for them to learn what responsibility means and how it is good for them to make responsible choices and decisions. It is not surprising therefore, that children are strangers to the field of responsibility as most adults would rather shirk it as well. Many people in wealthier societies live with coping mechanisms, going after material rewards and self-indulgence. How many of us are really interested in helping others, bettering society locally or globally. We are often so caught up in the net of our self-interest that we rarely think far beyond ourselves and our immediate circle of family and friends. Many of us are just living for the payoff; that is, winning the lottery with not much concern for others.

Bringing a larger sense of responsibility into our lives and the lives of our children helps us to rethink our deeper purpose in life. We take more responsibility in our lives; that is, beginning with our own happiness and the happiness of those around us, we start to see the immediate and surrounding conditions of our lives changing for the better. Accepting responsibility for our society at large, with even a small action such as picking up a piece of litter from the sidewalk and putting it in the trash, starts to demonstrate a real caring. We actually owe each other everything, in terms of providing the environment for ourselves and for others to maximize health, pleasure, personal growth and transformation. Providing an environment of responsibility and its subsequent benefits starts at home and expands to the world at large.

Anytime is a good time for children to learn the fine art of taking responsibility. Each generation learns to become responsible, to gear themselves toward lives of stability, accountability, and reliability. Children are waiting to be shown these skills, whether they acknowledge their need for responsibility or not. Children do demonstrate empathy at an early age but learning the skills of responsibility gives them the advantage of knowing how to act on empathetic feelings. Most children will not intuit how to act responsibly. Parents or teachers who are unskilled at teaching responsibility risk creating adults who are irresponsible and may impress children with their irresponsible behavior in negative ways. We may be raising new adults who are content to not accomplish much, to develop addictions, to have dysfunctional relationships, unfulfilling jobs, and all types of malaise. Children are just waiting for guidance, for instructions, for responsibility.

When parents, teachers and school administrators understand this deep seeking of responsibility in children, our progeny can really blossom in wholesome ways. Maria Montessori's school programs include many responsibility-inducing activities such as learning animal husbandry, personal grooming, putting things away, organized caring for the environment, for plants and animals. Montessori recognized in young children a drive toward both independence and responsibility. In most Montessori schools today, programs and activities are planned to cultivate the child's innate drive toward these two mutually supportive directions. Since children have this quest toward becoming independent and responsible, our task is to draw these qualities out of them and refine their abilities to fully understand and utilize responsibility while activating more and more of their inevitable independence. We are not inventing responsibilities in their lives. We are guiding and facilitating their natural drives.

Children usually do well when they are given the chance to accomplish something they value. That is, unless they have been discouraged by their earliest experiences to not release their gifts and talents. Most children really do want to help and want to be recognized for the help they give around the house and in school among their peers. Children often want to help parents clean up after a meal, to vacuum, to help parents around the house. They want to help with grocery shopping, with gardening, with watering plants. These seemingly mundane activities are actually fun for children and provide a proving ground for becoming responsible adults.

To live more fulfilling lives, responsibility should be cultivated. For children, responsibility should be cultivated from their earliest days. It is up to the adults who serve children—parents, relatives, neighbors, teachers—to themselves become more responsible, and then to pass on this vital skill.

Responsibility

- Incorporates and refines our overall abilities to care and love ourselves and others.
- Demonstrates the love within us toward the object of our responsibility.
- Demonstrates our responsiveness to others, to those we love, to those we serve.
- Allows us to be swept up in the grand dance of life, to its fullest so that we don't live mechanically like robots.
- Demonstrates our integrity in daily life, in situations of conflict where we are called to act for the purpose of the highest good.
- Helps us to make and keep commitments in thought, word and deed.
- Trains us to follow through to completion on those commitments.
- Gives us a sense of belonging but eschews attachment.
- Helps us become more present.
- Gives us a sense of accountability.

- Helps us define who we really care about in our lives, and even beyond our personal circles.

Children and Responsibility

In raising children, we apply all that we know about responsibility on a relative scale. Depending on the age of the child, their needs, skills and experience, we ascertain in each individual circumstance and situation how to impart the lessons of responsibility to the child.

We accept our roles in helping children become responsible to themselves, to others, to the environment and even to inanimate things. Following is a beginning list of activities you can use to cultivate responsibility in children. Feel free to be creative, to experiment and make up your own responsibilities. If these activities work well in teaching responsibility, please share your experiences with other parents and teachers.

Activities for Cultivating Responsibility in Children

- Help the child appreciate the value of putting toys away when finished, to clean up after themselves.
- Demonstrate how to follow through on activities the child begins so that projects are not abandoned capriciously.
- Teach the mechanics of activities that demonstrate responsibility.

Note: Even with toddlers, the adult can sit next to the child and guide their hands to put away food utensils, or even to clean up spills. Allow the child to hold a sponge and then with your adult hand over the child's hand, gently guide the process of wiping up a spill. Experiment with various techniques like this while determining if the child does not seem to be ready to engage in this way. It is always helpful to approach these teaching experiences with a sense of fun. As you observe results you can modify your techniques. Sometimes even waiting a few minutes during the learning process will teach you the best timing and approach to this important work. We are always in this process of developing responsible skills and habits with our children while at the same time developing our own expertise. Slowly we will begin to see the child understanding and valuing the order that responsibility brings. We can nurture a responsible child!

- Create physical places where the things that the child is responsible for go every time. It is necessary to have a place for everything the child will handle—from clothes to toys, to the food in the kitchen. Parents and teachers are encouraged to put up shelves, hooks, and organizing containers around the house and classroom. The child will then be better able to create order in their immediate world, to find where items belong and thereby reducing common frustrations and conflicts that come as a consequence of disorder. Putting things away becomes easy, a known quantity in the child's daily life. Routine is not a bad thing in learning these organizational skills on the path to responsibility.
- Let the child know what is expected of them. Expecting an orderly environment from the child helps them to experience harmony, balance, even beauty in both a conscious and an unconscious manner. This kind of natural order, not enforced, actually frees up emotional

and mental capacities for other important learning tasks ahead. As the child's brain is developing, the implications of order and responsibility are dramatic in the child's overall personal and social development.

- Teach the child not to blame others for their problems. Gently remind the child sometimes others do create problems for us and sometimes we are also complicit in creating our own problems. If the child can't find their rain boots, it doesn't necessarily mean that someone took them. It may mean that we forgot where we put them when we came into the classroom. Even if another child took a toy, we can learn to responsibly express our feelings in a safe way and even to allow for sharing of that toy. If someone is bullying us, again we can learn to responsibly express our feelings, and even eventually we can learn forgiveness. Good books are available as third-party tools to more impartially discuss these sometimes painful issues.

- Teaching the child about emotional reactions is a part of social emotional learning that inculcates responsibility in the child. If the child is feeling angry or sad or hurt, those emotions are genuine. However, we can teach that each of us has a choice of how to react emotionally to every circumstance or situation. We can teach that each of us is responsible for our emotions, for maintaining them, cultivating them or even choosing wiser ways to act and react. Playing various theatre and acting games with children is a proven way to allow them to rehearse different emotional options in a variety of situations.

- Avoid guilt. We don't want our children to develop guilt, but after a situation is understood and responsibilities have been analyzed together with the child, we want to help the child to feel that there is resolution through their acceptance of some responsibility in the incident that occurred. Excuses are heard but again, choice is emphasized. Help the child overcome tendencies toward feeling guilt or shame. And of course, avoid placing guilt or shame on the child. Do not threaten or criticize the child for their behavior as that will only deepen their inner wounds. We explain about apologizing, expressing contrition or remorse to an offended other party. If loving discipline is required, we fully explain the parameters. We tell that child, that in the future, we are confident that they will make better choices.
- Teaching responsible actions going forward from an incident. We can help children realize that they can go to the offended parties to resolve their conflicts themselves. Asking for forgiveness is difficult, but if we hold the child's hand (who is undertaking a positive action after some emotional incident) we will help in building their confidence and trust in attempting to right some wrong. The key here is that adults are meant to be children's allies, not their accusers. Our best intentions in teaching responsibility are always at the forefront.
- Teaching harmlessness. Children will eventually learn that responsibility means to be kind and loving to people, animals and plants. They learn that the responsibility to handle our own toys, books, clothes and devices, as well as those of others, means to be gentle and careful.

Some Final Thoughts on Responsibility

We learn and teach responsibility first through our own training. We learn to meditate on a regular basis, engage in physical exercise, maintain healthy personal and professional relationships, engage in fulfilling employment, eat right, absorb inspiring media such as uplifting books and films, find a community where we feel a wholesome kinship, and even develop a relationship of harmony and alignment with the Universe. Each day we set our purest intentions in the morning and try to implement those intentions as skillfully as possible. As we develop these skills, we also start to look outward to where we can be a more beneficial presence through our responsible thoughts, words and deeds thereby helping to create a more peaceful and just society for children and for ourselves worldwide.

Chapter 7
Integrity

> There are two ways in which you can hurt yourself:
>
> By reading or studying wisdom without being able to assimilate it.
>
> By reading and "understanding" wisdom without applying it in your life.
>
> In the first case you waste your time and money and fall into confusion. In the second case you create conflict and cleavages within you. But if you read and see the usefulness of the wisdom and then apply it to your life, you will become an integrated human being. Remember, "A house divided against itself cannot stand."
>
> – Torkom Saraydarian
> *The Ageless Wisdom*, pp. 33-4

Integrity is derived from the word *integer* which is a whole number, a number that is not a fraction. An integer is a thing complete in itself. Integrity is defined as the state of being whole and undivided. In more common usage, integrity denotes the quality of being honest and having strong moral principles or moral uprightness. Of what value is a person's character if they lack integrity?

Our integrity is the glue of our character. Integrity is character-strengthening. Our level of integrity makes us either congruent or virtuous in life or it makes us hypocrites. We can act in ways that are congruent with our best inner values or we can act against these. It is up to us.

Children often are raised among adults who are saying by their example, "Do as I say, not as I do." When impressionable children observe the discrepancies between our words and our actions, they learn to be hypocrites. Do we want to raise another generation of confused, lost searchers? Again, it is up to us as parents and educators to choose the best path for our children.

It is a tall order to become an integral person. It is a tall order to reshape our behavior. This actually calls for a creative yet thorough reshaping of our entire lives. How many of us are committed enough to the quality of our lives and our family's lives to work diligently to change ourselves? Yet, such changes are a must. If we stay the same and behave with the same habits, we will reap the same bleak rewards—a world on the edge of destruction along with a mass culture of crime, war, and perpetual fear.

It is up to us to change the fabric of society. Of course, this begins with the baby steps of our own individual change and transformation.

Living with Integrity

How do we become more integral beings? We can begin by choosing to keep our word. We can begin by making ourselves follow through on our commitments. If we discover that these commitments are outdated or inappropriate at this time, we can practice the principle of renegotiation. We can take it upon ourselves to renegotiate our former commitments and to reshape them into appropriate agreements congruent with our ideal selves. We can learn to negotiate and renegotiate with others. This not only improves our skills in human interaction but it also teaches our subconscious mind that when difficulties emerge, they can be overcome. Face to face, by negotiating, by teaching ourselves to resolve conflicts, and to live and act with friends and even opponents, we can find the spirit of goodwill for real concordance.

Our willpower effectively can be used to change ourselves. We must make a conscious and sincere decision to change. Next, we must make the efforts necessary to maintain these changes. We are actually reeducating ourselves to reshape our former ways of acting into integral ways! This takes an inner resolve and a strength of determination. It requires an act of will on our part. Yet, if we do this, we will be upgrading our life skills tremendously, becoming truly eligible to parent or to educate children.

Our integrity demonstrates itself in our behavior. It reveals itself through our words, feelings and thinking, and of course, our actions. Our level of integrity shows up in our every move. Our children and those close to us either reap the rewards of our behaviors or they face unseen sabotage. Following is an inventory of journal, contemplation, and discussion questions that may be used for deeper insight and self-awareness on the path to becoming more whole integral beings.

Integrity Questions
- Do we keep our word to others, to our families, to our co-workers and supervisors, to our neighbors and relatives?
- Are we to be taken at our word?

- Should others trust us?
- Are we trustworthy?
- What are our truest motives?
- Do we follow through on our agreements?
- Do we generally support others, or let them down?
- How do we respond under pressure?
- How do we respond when we know others are counting on us?
- How do we handle ourselves in positions of responsibility?
- Are we pleased with our behavior, past and present?
- What would we like to do differently?
- What is our ideal behavior?
- What is our broadest vision for the future?
- What would we like to do differently in the future?

These are important, penetrating questions for us to be asking ourselves, and answering honestly. We have a valuable opportunity to examine ourselves, deeply and sincerely at any moment. We can begin to process this self-inquiry by journaling about integrity issues. We may ask others for insights into their observed behaviors of us, including our own parents, children, and spouses. And yes, we may even ask reflections from those people who we suspect may have negative reports about us. We must be open to seeing the truth about ourselves, facing even unpleasant truths.

Our level of integrity can always be upgraded. Changing ourselves is an "inside job." It starts and ends with our own efforts. Others can help us by being our mirrors but inevitably we are responsible for ourselves to become whole individuals. We do children a service by presenting them with this holistic approach to life, encouraging personal responsibility and courage through our own demonstration of integral words and actions. As always, children live what they learn.

Chapter 8
Contentment

If we think about it, our lives are made more fulfilling by our positive attitudes. Negativity and criticism undermine our joy, success and contentment. It is a fact that when we think of the things that we do not like or approve of, we create a negative atmosphere around us. Contentment is just the opposite of this. Contentment is defined as a condition or state of happiness and satisfaction, a sense of fulfillment. Contentment is not a self-indulgent or conceited state but rather it is a feeling that everything is alright and we can relax into the present moment, while of course staying alert into the next moment. We can even play with the word contentment, emphasizing content; intimating, that one who is content has a certain positive and fulfilling containment of their faculties and actions.

When a parent is content, this feeling overflows to the home and family. It seems obvious that when we are content, joy follows. If we really want more fulfilling lives, we would do well to first consider upgrading our outlook on life. We start toward the goal of finding contentment right where we are. If we are not pleased with current circumstances, we have the ability to change them. On a very real level, "our destiny is in our hands."

Here are our main options: Either we choose to focus on the positive in the here and now; meaning that we accept, appreciate and even praise this moment or, if we want to make changes by taking our destiny into our own hands, we do so.

Both are valid options in seeking contentment, ultimately creating a happy life for ourselves, our families, our communities and the international community. Choosing to find joy in any situation breeds the contentment that leads to joy.

If we become too concerned with outward appearances and spend too little time creating wholesome attitudes, we cannot find contentment. Converting our negative thoughts into positive ones will result in outward appearances automatically improving for us. Approach each day with good expectations and good things just seem to follow. Not much of this simply falls into our laps. We have to reach up and out. Expect great things! Work for great things. Contentment always follows our best volitions.

A positive outlook can bring positive results in our quest for contentment but our outlook isn't the only factor. Real action must follow our positive outlook, both working together. We can learn to focus on the positive in life, even without sticking our heads in the sand, denying those things which are cruel and unacceptable. We are not overlooking the negative but with the eyes of love, we look for the paths to contentment. These are skills that we also want to pass on to children.

Reframing our Thoughts

We can find and practice techniques for becoming content. Below are some places where we can begin this important journey to contentment while learning to drop thoughts and attitudes that no longer work for us. We replace negative, discontent-producing complaints, grievances and criticisms with more positive, life-affirming thoughts and balanced attitudes. Below are some steps we can take in our path toward inner contentment.

- When we catch ourselves doing, thinking, feeling, or saying things we know we will later regret, we can stop ourselves midstream, and reverse these actions.
- Reflecting on a past event or circumstance where we thought, spoke or acted in some harsh or unskilled manner, at a later quiet time or even at a retreat, we can return in our imaginations to the event, and rethink it or reimagine how we would produce a more favorable interaction or outcome. This technique helps us overcome stored guilt, anger, jealousy, grief, or even revenge.
- A similar technique that is also helpful in eliminating negative memories and thus restoring contentment is called the Evening Review. Before retiring at night, we find some quiet time alone and mentally return to the day's events: Beginning with the present moment in the evening, we visualize ourselves going back through the day in reverse order, ending with the moment we arose in the morning. When we come to a moment where we wish we would have reacted differently—with different words or emotions—we again mentally rework this episode. We picture ourselves doing what we now wish we had done to get a more favorable outcome.

These helpful techniques return us to a present state of contentment. We can restore joy, self-trust, and confidence in ourselves and our most treasured ideals. We begin to see more clearly how we created our own discontent. At the same time, we reaffirm that our very essence is greater than our behaviors. Again, we reflect on the realization that we are the creators of our lives and experiences, that we individually can choose contentment or discontent.

Further, these techniques help us to somewhat distance the 'real me'—that person who seeks to act according to their highest ideals—from the untoward events and experiences we pass through in our lives. We come to find that we are not our experiences, that we are not our thoughts, feelings, and actions. Rather, the reactions to events and circumstances allow us the opportunities to choose whether to move from the core of 'real me' and choose that which ultimately achieves the most wholesome and holistic sense of contentment for ourselves and others. From these understandings and practices, we then move on authentically to work with our children using similar techniques and providing real guidance to them along their own paths to contentment, true happiness, peace, and joy.

Chapter 9
Courage

When courage radiates outward, it wipes away all fear because at the moment of its flow, you are at the center of your true being and not identified with your physical, emotional and mental nature. When you are truly your Self, fear does not exist for you.

Each courageous one who comes to the world, such as Socrates, Gandhi or Christ, uplifts the whole world to a higher degree of understanding and cooperation. Courage must expand and involve the whole. If it does not expand, it turns into selfishness, cruelty, crime, and destroys itself.

Before a person reaches the full expression of courage, he learns to welcome blows on behalf of others. He stands for the true rights of others; he protects them from any kind of evil attack but he does this without expectation. Through such a life, he eventually stands within his own inner Light.

Courage cannot be attained in one day. You work for it for centuries. Every little act of selfless service, every little act of welcoming risks on behalf of others, slowly carries you up.

An act of courage is not an act of foolishness. A true act of courage carries a deep wisdom, a clear discrimination and a developed skill-in-action.

Steel is tested by fire, but the strength of spirit grows through the breath of life.

– Torkom Saraydarian
The Psyche & Psychism, pp. 970 - 972

Courage

The Latin derivative of courage is *cor,* meaning heart and denoting the seat of feelings. In usage, it has come to signify the ability to do something that frightens one. Courage is an outstanding virtue to cultivate in this challenging age. When people develop courage as children, they will carry it with them everywhere. It will be a vital, empowering life ingredient. Parents give children a great gift when they inspire courage within them. Courage is the flower of our own inner experiences and labor. It grows from testing our strengths and weaknesses in the arena of daily life. We develop courage only by allowing ourselves to explore, experiment, and even fail. As we learn to dive fearlessly into the waters of life, we develop courage. As we take more risks physically, emotionally, and mentally, we develop courage. We also broaden ourselves by surpassing our former limitations.

Courage is like the crown of victory that is won by the striving spirit. Children gain courage as they meet their own obstacles and difficulties and stand up to them. We all gain courage this way. Our victories give us added confidence to proceed with even more courage throughout life. Our successes give us courage. Yet, our mistakes can also facilitate our courage. When we fail, we must courageously get up again and persevere. Children may have difficulty attaining courage if parents give them negative messages about failure. Most of us believe that failure has no value in human development and maturity. We seek a perfect world where we are not challenged much, where we never get dirt on us. Yet, the fact is that the dust and grit of life does come upon us. Life is filled with its trials and challenges. And every trial or tribulation requires our courage and ingenuity to overcome those challenges. If we want to accomplish our goals in life, we need courage. If we want to do well and contribute to life, we must have courage. If we want to improve ourselves and the quality of life in general, courage is required. If we want to enter into partnerships and close personal relationships, we must have courage.

We need courage for just about everything! Every initiative we make and every step forward requires an act of some degree of courage. Fearful people spend their lives spinning their wheels, procrastinating, making excuses and do not leave the world with much of a contribution. Living as a giver of life, not just a taker, requires discrimination and wisdom to make good choices and decisions. Recklessness and inappropriate risk-taking are not considered to be acts of courage. Courage is to be applied to those tasks which are deemed to require appropriate actions, challenging as they are. When life requires something of us, we must get up the courage to perform.

It is difficult for children to build their courage when they are surrounded by fearful adults. When the child's environment is filled with fear and inhibitions, taboos, and strict regulations, they will learn to conform to the status quo or be motivated to break positive societal rules. The child will not develop into an independent, creative person. The child will not gain autonomy nor likely develop much creativity. It is unlikely that a fearful child will learn to think with originality. These developmental traits lead to low self-esteem and a lack of confidence. A fearful environment, no matter how masked or subtle, will produce a fearful, constricted person. This is the antithesis of courage.

When we are courageous, we push ourselves to surpass our limits. We are focused on a goal that leads to success. We live for excellence. We are persistent. We become lifelong strivers. We apply effort, imagination and skill in everything we do. Of course, courage makes demands on us. Wallowing in outdated ways of living may seem easy but eventually it extracts a big price from us. Courage requires exertion, and that exertion rewards us tenfold.

Remember, children are growing up watching our every move so we really owe it to them to work toward virtues like courage in our own lives, at the same time encouraging them to understand the concepts and practice of courage. We do not want to encourage our children to just develop coping mechanisms, simply to be plugging along in life. We want to demonstrate how to overcome our perceived limitations. When we do this, we are parenting and educating with purpose and integrity. The future will inherit the gifts of well-raised children, reared by striving parents.

Our courage and our children's courage paves the way for personal growth and transformation. As we refine our children's traits towards the ideals we espouse, we eventually see our children bloom as mature human beings. Exercising courage inspires a holistic vision for a greater collective good. Courage is motivated by an underlying sense of unity. As the nature of courage deepens within us, we achieve greater empathy, compassion, generosity and love, thereby truly moving ever nearer to the heart of the highest feelings we can express for ourselves and others.

Courage allows us to imagine the unity of the whole of mankind, along with the creation of a greater understanding between nations and between the various kingdoms of nature.

Courage requires a fearless attitude. Fearlessness can and must be cultivated. Usually, it does not come naturally to us. We must develop and refine it within ourselves. Everywhere we are bombarded by rules and images which restrict our courage and spontaneity. To become truly creative and industrious, we must ignore these boundaries, surpassing them in daily life. This is the road to a future culture based upon beauty, genius, and unlimited progress. We can begin to actualize it by seeing courage as one of the biggest catalysts for changing our lives. And again, for children to actualize courage, they must have it revealed to them through us as well as through their own independent experiences in life.

Courage Workbook

- List the areas and topics in which you want to develop more courage.
- Become aware of the areas in which fear still rules in your life.
- Locate the ways this fear is holding you back and limiting you from accomplishing what you wish.
- Discover and list what you think these fears are costing you.
- Are you ready to overcome these? How ready are you?
- What do you plan to do about this?
- Develop a plan of action, a strategy for overcoming fears, one by one.
- Journal about your expanding courage. Discuss your experiences with trusted people. Investigate habits and lifestyles that block or sabotage courage.
- Keep in mind the road to courage is not easy, as the Lion in the *Wizard of Oz* discovered.

Chapter 10
Giving

Generosity is a great sign of nobility.
      – Torkom Saraydarian
      The Psyche and Psychism, p. 1103

Sacrifice is a response to a great vision which the disciple catches and is gradually absorbed in. This absorption in the vision reaches to such a degree that he gives all that he is and he has to actualize his vision. Sacrificial energy pours out from the core of his being and clears away all that stands on the way to their vision.
      – *Ibid.*, p. 1096

My heart I give to thee, O Lord. Sacrifice it for the sake of the world.

      Leaves of Morya's Garden, Vol. I, para. 317

Giving and Sacrifice

Giving, true giving, is behind all good relationships. This holds true for the relationships between parents and children, and between parents and schools. True giving is giving without expectations. Giving for the sheer joy of giving; giving because it is our duty to give; giving because it is perhaps the most heroic way we can behave in a situation. Giving is inexhaustible. It can exist forever and in infinite varieties.

Why is this a topic in a book about children? Because children are perhaps the prime candidates to receive all the giving that we can offer them. Children need all the good that we can give them. They need what we have to offer them. They need love, freedom to grow and develop, and they need the space in which to do all this.

Since children are such active doers, we must be active givers in order to be supportive to them in their development.

Of course, we also have needs. We do. Yet, to be optimal parents and role models for children, and to provide the most supportive environments for them, we must also find creative ways to meet our own needs. This means that adults must be resourceful and also as mature as possible. And we all know that maturity, acting responsibly towards others and ourselves, is an ongoing process.

We can make ourselves happy and find fulfillment on our own. Then, from our own position of relative autonomy, we will not rely on our children to give us happiness and fulfillment, or to validate us. We are not looking to them to meet our needs. It is from our own position of relative inner security and strength that we are prepared to become givers to our children. We can only give to them and to others from our own inner strength. As long as we lean or depend on others, our children included, we are weak and are a source of weakness.

At every moment, we can either give or take. The reader may have questions about what we mean by giving. For purposes of illustration here, let us allow this point to be put in black and white. All of us know on some level when we are giving or taking, when we are serving or are concerned with reaping some benefit for ourselves. We either know this blatantly or on some level our consciences tell us. We are either contributing to a situation or taking away from it. We are either in support of a person and are their ally or we are robbing them of our support. Of course, our behavior and the support we demonstrate to them will vary. Sometimes on the surface we may appear to be giving in a certain situation when, in fact, we very subtly are taking from that situation. If we are in the giving mode, we are absorbed in the ways that contribute and transform for the greater good. Then we are filled with goodwill and we have the concerns of another close to ours. We may even experience joy as we are wrapped up in giving and serving.

If we are caught up more in taking, then we are more concerned with ourselves and our self-interest. We are more absorbed with our interests at the expense of others. This is a subtle and tricky point because we are not always aware of when we are doing something at someone else's expense. When we do things at the expense of others, we are taking. Yet most of us are professionals at self-deception. We find it easy to tell ourselves that we can listen to our children and spouses with half an ear while we watch TV or do the laundry. If we do things that rob others of our attention, or rob them of affection, courtesy, or love at the appropriate times, we are taking. When we are giving, we are absorbed with that giving and very much present in the moment. When we are giving, we are asking ourselves how we can support and serve the other person, even trying to find ways to sacrifice something to meet the other's needs.

Sacrifice, as a word or as a subject, has nowadays come under immense controversy. Many people even resent hearing about sacrifice. They feel they will lose something, and that to give something to someone else is to override their own needs, assuring that they will come out losers. This is the kind of thinking that limits people. It limits families, groups and even nations. False notions of sacrifice claim that by giving, we lose. This has never been true. Even the great thinkers of the ages have written, "To give is to receive." When we are truly giving, we feel that we as the giver and the receiver are truly connected. We become united with the receiver in a special sort of way.

Considering the power of our being givers, in relation to our children and families, to our coworkers, to our relationships with schools and teachers is truly foundational. Children must learn this fundamental life tenet first from us as early childhood caregivers. The understanding and activation of giving is the most wholesome way for children to reap the deepest spiritual and, ultimately, material rewards of life. When we say we care, we really strive to prepare our children with these fundamentals. Giving more time and attention to our own needs and hobbies, our favorite TV programs, our time off, our own careers, friends, relationships, and love lives, we run the risk of being hypocritical in our stated intentions. When we say we are givers, and then do not make constant, sincere efforts to give our children what they truly need, lots of times at our own expense, we need to reexamine our own fundamental intentions. When we call ourselves generous and claim to be serving our children, yet deny them things that are important to them, such as field trips, driving to see their friends, sleepover parties, healthy and well-prepared meals, and quality time with them, we are forgetting our duties and our noblest goals in raising truly happy and strong children. Our denial of their needs ensures that we are taking from them.

It is time for us to recommit ourselves to giving. To commit ourselves to giving 100%. This is a lifelong process; let's not kid ourselves. We are all in the process of becoming more giving and more loving. Let us make the most of this incredible opportunity awarded to us by life—the opportunity to give, to serve, and to love! It all starts with changing ourselves and upgrading our own lives. Next, it spreads out to our children and families, and eventually to our world.

Chapter 11
Tenderness

> In tenderness you build bridges between you and other living beings, and through these bridges your soul reaches them. In brutality you build walls and destroy bridges. You make your service for others impossible.
>
> In tenderness, your compassion expands and your wisdom fills your chalice. Brutality uses the mind; tenderness uses the heart.
>
> One can learn many secrets of tenderness by watching how certain children express it toward almost everything they touch or relate with.
>
> – Torkom Saraydarian
> *Challenge for Discipleship*, pp. 260-1

When we speak of tenderness, we are talking about the feeling of gentleness and kindness, the feeling of affection and concern, and warmth.

Children respond to people who treat them tenderly and with love. Tenderness is a characteristic which has been like a diamond in the rough—it is only now beginning to receive press. Tenderness for others may be one of the most important gifts we can give. Children thrive on tenderness. So do our close relationships. To be tender is a skill that we can develop from within ourselves. It does not mean that we give up our strength and personal power. On the contrary, the strongest and most secure people are oftentimes the most tender people.

To be tender with others, and especially with our children and families, does not mean that we give up our ability to uphold the ground rules or to maintain order. It does not mean that we lose respect in the eyes of others. On the contrary, we come closer to the light of love.

There are times to be tender. There are times to be strong. There are times to be strict. There are times to be more forceful. There are times we may seek to use tough love with our children, though there is a very fine line between tough love and forceful discipline. The ultimate form of discipline is when we help the child to monitor and correct themselves from within. This is the ideal and grows over time, cultivated by patience on the part of all who serve the child. Tenderness exists whether we are in an overt discipline mode with children or not.

Tenderness is really an energy which can animate our entire behavior, our entire outlook, words, and thoughts. It can penetrate into our entire life, filling it with hope, aliveness, vitality, and greater love. With tenderness and kindness—a form of gentleness also—coloring all of our behavior, we create the atmosphere for healthy relationships both at home and school. This is really what children need to develop into healthy adults. Tenderness is also something that most of us are seeking from our relationships. If we think about this wonderful quality more deeply, it is what our world needs for a foundation of health and beauty. Tenderness is not a weak behavior.

Those who do not want to, or cannot, embrace tenderness as a basic necessity for a healthy life will intentionally or unintentionally be adding to the problems arising within our families, schools and society. Such problems naturally overflow into our world at large.

Thus, in a very real sense, we owe it to ourselves, to our community, and especially to our children, to provide environments filled with a tenderness that engenders joy, love, hope, and beauty. Exercising tenderness in every situation or circumstance that we come across with our children goes a long way toward fulfilling the goal of holistic parenting and educating children.

Chapter 12
Patience

> A whole civilization can be built upon the principle of patience.
>
> – Torkom Saraydarian
> *The Psyche and Psychism*, p. 1027

Children thrive in an atmosphere of patience, and adults who truly understand the value of patience give a loving and vital gift to children. Most of us want to be with people who give us a chance to be who we are and to speak freely without interruption. We enjoy interacting with those who trust us, and those who allow us our idiosyncrasies and quirks. We want to be with people who are patient and who treat us patiently. Let us outline the components of patience; that is, what patience is and is not, the value of patience and the purposes it serves, and what brings patience into being within us and within our families and lives.

Patience is…

- Trusting the other person and believing in them.
- Letting things, life and events unfold.
- Waiting, and becoming acclimated to waiting.
- Tolerating.
- Withholding our judgments and not jumping to conclusions.

- Maintaining a wholesome vision despite appearances.
- Knowing the value of time.
- Becoming process-oriented, more than goal-oriented.
- Overlooking so-called faults and weaknesses in others.
- Not hurrying.
- Trusting time.
- Developing a sense of right timing.
- Optimism in life and its processes.
- Steadfastness.
- Perseverance.
- Staying on purpose despite distractions.
- Reticence in speech.
- Quietness and confidence.
- Carrying burdens because of love.
- Manifesting inner strength.
- Appropriate waiting.
- Knowing that things will be resolved.
- Commitment and loyalty.
- Not rushing to fix or change things.
- Demonstrating respect.
- Allowing people to be free to be themselves.
- Learning not to interfere.
- Acknowledging that things develop in due time.
- Realizing that we must earn certain things in life.
- Serenity.
- Giving.
- Trust.
- Inner and outer calmness.
- Forgiveness.

- Giving the benefit of the doubt.
- Maintaining inner stability by being grounded.
- Having the ability to wait.
- Seeing a vision of what is possible as completed.
- Seeking to help when needed.
- Not limiting others.
- Developing and maintaining faith and hope.
- Ability to delay gratification and the satisfaction of ones' needs.

The Value and Purpose of Patience

When we are patient, we have an inherent understanding of a person and their life. Once we understand another person, deeply and sincerely, we can let go and be patient with them. We can stand back to let things be and unfold. Without this understanding, we feel the need to rush, to push, and to force our own wills onto situations. Without understanding, we will not be patient. We will not be perceiving a person or an event as it is in its entire manifestation. Instead, we will project our needs, fears and motives onto others, and we will feel the need to force, cajole, and manipulate. We will be operating from our egos, not from deep understanding.

Anytime we feel the need to manipulate, we must examine our own belief systems and fears. What causes these fears? What if our fears turned out to be true? What if the worst fear were to happen? As we gain deeper understanding of our own fears and the fears of others, we can begin to develop a space to develop greater patience!

The Values and Purpose of Patience

- Allows others to be themselves, deterring our interference.
- Allows situations to be, to unfold, and develop at their own pace.
- Encourages and sustains our freedom of choice within situations.
- Develops a healthy detachment from fear and dependency.
- Frees us from emotional bondage and dependency on conditions.
- Frees us from forcing our wills on others.

Patience with Children

It is important for them to be exposed to patience as early as possible; that is, to be taught patience, to have patience modeled for them, and for children to live with patience. Our patience with children lets them know that they are important. We let them know that we always have the time to listen— really listen—to them.

- Demonstrating patience with a child's projects is worth our full and undivided attention.
- We are demonstrating respect and cherishing for the child.
- We learn to really receive from the child.
- We are open to the child as we allow ourselves to be taught by them.
- We allow ourselves to be the child's servants, in service to their development.

- We are receptive to the child's needs.
- We encourage the child to unfold and develop at their own pace.
- We help the child to develop in their own unique ways.
- We don't hurry the child.
- We give the child the message that they are special and that they count.
- We let the child know they are worthy in taking our time with them.
- We appreciate the child in their inherent process orientation in life.
- We role model adults' caring and listening.

Catalysts for Adult Patience

- Wanting to further develop my capacity for patience.
- Acknowledging the value of patience.
- Life experiences that cause me to become patient.
- Tests and challenges that help me to become patient.
- Knowing that a child becomes patient when it has been modeled for them.
- Creating a home environment with adult models that demonstrate patience.
- Having and keeping a wholesome vision helps us become more patient.
- Seeing that teaching ourselves patience helps us to manifest it.
- Admiring patience in others helps transform us.
- Learning through experience the follies of impatience.
- Experiencing how haste creates problems.

- Finding an accepting attitude within us develops patience.
- Understanding the hearts of others and the problems of others.
- Searching for ways to become patient.
- Understanding the healing power of time.

When to Practice Patience

Children give us many opportunities to exercise patience. Following are some examples of occasions in which our patience may be tested, and where we may begin to change some former habits of impatience.

- When the child does not clean their rooms.
- When the child does not follow through on duties and responsibilities.
- When you have asked the child to turn off the TV and join you for dinner.
- When the child is procrastinating.
- When the child is taking longer than you feel is appropriate to put their things away.
- When the young child is clumsy at cleaning up spills, either with your help or without.
- When the child is changing their clothes, or getting ready for bed.
- When the child is prolonging their morning rituals in getting ready for school.
- When you are listening to the child.
- While you are talking with the child.
- During explanations, either yours or the child's.

Activities to Help Practice Patience

These are helpful techniques for overcoming guilt, and for educating ourselves for future experiences in places where we will want to exercise patience.

- Intend to be patient.
- Stop midstream, while you are wanting to act impatiently. Then, reword your words and/or change your behavior.
- When you notice that you are thinking impatiently or acting impatiently, slow down and change your course.
- Demonstrate your sincerity and your commitment with mindfulness practice!
- In private time, recall occasions when you were impatient.
- Think of the situation, without becoming angry or guilty.
- Seek to discover the reasons you were impatient.
- What really caused you to act impatiently? (Irritation, agitation, self-righteousness?)
- Do not judge yourself or become harsh with yourself.
- How could you have acted differently.
- See yourself and the entire situation as if you are a stranger looking at it.
- Mentally, act out how you would change the impatient behavior.
- Look for times and places in your daily life where you can practice being more patient in your words, thoughts, feelings, actions, and intentions.
- Work mentally through a possible challenging situation in the future with your family, children, co-workers and strangers.

- See yourself successful and victorious in being patient.
- See those around you benefitting from your patience and being happy.
- Feel a sense of happiness and accomplishment within yourself from these exercises.

There is an ancient idea that when we act *as if* we were already embodying a certain desirable frame of mind, we actually help ourselves become transformed into our ideal self! A more modern saying goes, "Fake it till you make it." Either way, once we know our behavioral goals, we have a vision. Once we have a vision, we can begin to take the steps necessary to move toward that vision. Since changing our behavior really starts with a shift of belief systems, find some beliefs and attitudes you hold which work against you acting patiently with others. These belief systems would need to change in order to become more patient.

Be creative and create more of your own activities to develop and enhance greater patience. Our efforts in these directions eventually bear fruit. You will see the fruits of your labors if you work patiently!

Chapter 13
Trust

As soon as you trust yourself, you will know how to live.
– Goethe

If a child lives with security, he learns to have faith.
– D.L. Nolte

Why is trust such an important feature in our lives, and in the lives of children? Trust promotes healthy relationships. When children learn trust, they can make friends with life, with the world, and they can make friends throughout the world. Trust enables children to become givers, and to not live in fear. Fear is the opposite of trust and causes much pain in the world. Faith is a by-product of trust. Self-trust is the foundation for a happy life.

We experience trust in various ways. We can trust ourselves, trust others, trust events and trust the process of life itself. This may be a radical view for some people. When we trust ourselves, we make decisions that we can respect and that we can back up. When we trust ourselves, we respect ourselves. Trust means that we are not plagued with indecisiveness, undue caution or inhibitions to express our creativity. We are more alive, spontaneous, and authentic in our approach to life. We become willing to do new things, make new discoveries, branch out and take certain risks. When we are self-trusting, we are more creative in the lives that we make for ourselves. Trust means that we are not living as robots, mechanically but in an open and organic way.

Trust is the foundation for successful relationships. When we trust the people with whom we are closely involved, we succeed in our relationships with them. And we inspire mutual trust, caring, and respect.

We feel good when we are trusted. When we are not trusted, we live in a state of constant tension and suspicion, no matter how subtle. No one likes to live "under the gun," always being suspected of some misdeeds. Living with suspicion, of other people or events, turns us into machines of pessimism, negativity, and even paranoia. This is not to say that we must be naïve about life, looking at life through rose-colored glasses. Of course, we should be attentive to the people and events playing out in our lives, observing everything with an attentive eye. However, allowing all the processes we witness and we participate in to be filtered through the lens of our optimism, we have the ability to keep a positive mental attitude.

If we live in a constant state of mistrust our lives are doomed to suffering. Mistrust eats away at our motivation, success, and health. When we mistrust, our lives eventually reflect this state of being. From a weedy garden good things do not grow. We owe it to ourselves to pull out the weeds that prevent us from living optimistic, hopeful, and loving lives.

The child is born with trust. But a child can lose trust quickly in the face of life's earliest challenges. After several negative or painful experiences, a child's trust factor becomes whittled away, they begin to protect themselves and to live cautiously. Such distrust as a behavioral pattern does not need to continue through the child's life. When we, as early childhood caregivers recognize the value of trust and openness, we can help recreate trust for a damaged child as an individual, within the family structure, and in the child's broader world. Then, developing as an adult—in business, relationships and community—trust can be instilled again in the individual who had negative early experiences, eroding their trust. Dysfunctional belief systems can be made whole and well again. We can find the opportunity for healing and strength in any given situation, and ultimately see the potential for growth and transformation. The child who was hurt early on can learn forgiveness and release the past.

Trust and forgiveness of course are intimately connected. It can be said that every damaged relationship is eroded from broken trust. Learning and practicing forgiveness helps us restore the comfort, love, and balance in our relationships that trust gives us. Trust is not just a mental function. It is a function of the feeling part of our heart. If we approach the issue of trust with our minds alone, we may never move in the direction of actual trust. We will likely stay stuck in our modes of fear, caution and suspicion. The mind does not readily trust. We are both defensive by nature mentally and physically but we also understand intrinsically the necessity of trust in our daily lives. Ultimately, trusting others and trusting life requires a heartfelt leap of faith, even within a society that encourages competition and material gain.

If we look at the beauty and innocence of children at their earliest stages of development, they can teach us much in the area of trust. Initially there is a natural tendency toward trust by the child based on their trusting relationship with their first caregivers. When that natural trust is expressed by the child, it is truly a wonderful experience for adults too. Children can trust and give unconditionally. This is one of the greatest gifts and memories that children give to adults, that natural and authentic quality of trust that we adults so often seek again as we experience more of the cynical and bitter experiences of adult life.

When we are always protecting our self-serving interests, there will be elements of fear that we are experiencing and that we are expressing to others that do not contribute to our own need for trust, nor for others who also seek trust. When we can demonstrate trust, overcoming our urge for unreasonable safety guarantees, we begin to make breakthroughs in human relations. This does not mean we "throw all cares to the wind."

Discrimination and wisdom are always needed in assessing people and events. At the same time, we need to be aware of habitual patterns where we protect ourselves, even at another person's expense. Trust is both a goal and a process, for both adults and children.

> No one can really advance in a higher search if the foundation on which he stands is not shaken and destroyed. You need a crisis to make a breakthrough. The wind and the storm must come and hit your existence and test your foundation.
> – Torkom Saraydarian
> *The Flame of Beauty, Culture, Love,* Joy, p. 182

Chapter 14
Persistence and Perseverance

If we want to succeed in anything, we must persist. Children, especially young children, tend to have very short attention spans. They tend to give up easily. Many children get bored easily. By our own example and by using creative means, adults can teach children about the virtues of persistence. We want to help our children learn that nothing of real value can be accomplished without persisting, putting out real energy and effort for a valuable cause. Persistence is 99% of success, as the old saying goes. We adults understand that human life is filled with challenges and that we have to face these challenges. Persistence in overcoming our trials and tribulations is the primary factor in tackling challenges by whatever means we use to persevere over these challenges. The earlier a child is empowered with this knowledge, the earlier the mental, emotional, physical and spiritual powers of the child are developed for the long haul.

The great heroes of culture and civilization, both ancient and modern, make for inspiring reading. Children's books about the lives and accomplishments of heroic people provide models of persistence and perseverance to young readers. Wholesome film, TV, and other media that portray high motivations and methods (that the hero uses to overcome even insurmountable odds) help the child envision the endless possibilities that life offers those who have vision, are brave, and don't give up. Role models help the child even to see the heroes that exist or previously existed among family, friends, and the community, in sports, the arts, and politics. Whether fictional or real, we can use every story— metaphorical, mythological, real-life, even spiritual— that reveal to the child examples of how very often even just plain folk accomplish great things using the amazing quality of persistence.

As parents, caregivers, or educators, naturally we want to help our children when things get tough for them. This may be a wrong sort of training. Not allowing the child to struggle, even to fail, can create an unrealistic world view for the child. We adults know that failure, disillusionment and despair do exist in life. To teach perseverance means to facilitate a great vision of each situation, allowing answers to come from the child. Encouraging goals can hearten and cheer the child by urging that innate but difficult quality of persistence to be activated and increased as the child gets each step closer to their goal.

The old adage that arises here: Show, don't tell. By your own example in the child's daily life, your steadfastness in any project radiates strength, endurance, stamina, self-confidence and the patience that demonstrates how one perseveres and eventually prevails in any project or situation. At the same time that we teach and demonstrate all of these wonderful qualities, there may be a time when we actually hit a dead end, and there truly is nothing more to be done. There is a time to accept things as they are and to see and appreciate the value of the lessons we learned along the way. Sometimes it *is* time to capitulate, and yet much has been accomplished in our process and with our persistence.

The lessons of persistence demonstrate to children how their active and dynamic commitment to a worthy goal activates their innate powers of choice and decision making.

We teach our children that if you "stick it out" during stressful times, success eventually manifests. We teach that the qualities of patience and belief in our vision, and activating all our willpower are needed during the intense periods of doubt and delay that are part of the hero's weapons (or tools) in attaining victory over the greater odds of defeat.

Perseverance is a matter of inner decision and inner activation. It is not something that simply happens to us. It does not come from outside us, though we can be inspired by outside events or persons, even cheered on by others. Again, it is the individual (or the team) that actually makes all the great stuff happen. We make our decisions and commitments, then create the causes and conditions which produce the results. All this occurs within the field of persistence.

So, whatever project the child embarks on, we help them get excited about it. We encourage the child not to drop those qualities that are needed on the journey. We can point out the strengths and assets that we need to hone to accomplish our goals, as well as the qualities that we already possess within us or outside of us as material resources. We keep in mind that dream or vision throughout our trek. We begin, step by step, on the road to our goal. If there is a false start, or a wrong few steps, we back up and begin anew. We are continually refreshing the page (to use a computer term), discarding what is not needed, thereby providing a clean slate. There is no guilt for pausing and considering new options or directions. We just continue enthusiastically. We just persist and persevere, and we discover what we have needed to know, what the real lessons are that life wants to teach us. Our creative muscles are flexed and invigorated. We go for it! And we see how our persistence and perseverance finally "lifts all boats," making a difference that contributes mightily to a wholesome life for ourselves, our families, our communities and for the entire global society. Persistence makes the difference and it brings the results!

Chapter 15
Humility

> Humility is the awareness that nothing belongs to you. You do not even belong to yourself. All great things that you do are a process of transmission from the One Life which animates us all to itself.
>
> Humility decentralizes you and makes you feel that you are one with the whole. You are a blooming flower on a tree. Humility gives you patience toward your own limitations and toward the limitations of others.
>
> Humility prepares a person to be a future hero.
>
> – Torkom Saraydarian
> *The Psyche and Psychism*, pp. 934,937

It is difficult to teach a child humility when we are vain. It's difficult to demonstrate humility when we think we are better than others; when we are puffed up with self-importance; when we are selfish and self-centered.

Humility comes only when we let go of our limiting thoughts, fears, and egoism, when we stand above our limiting egos. It has been said that when we stand with the spirit of the warrior in order to conquer our own limitations, we will be victorious. Even if we are not immediately or technically "victorious," our efforts toward mastery in the form of humility are themselves worthy of our acknowledgment as these efforts are supported by life itself, and these efforts do count toward self-mastery.

Humility is the capacity to put on hold our need to control people, situations, and outcomes. This need to control manifests out of our fears and from our seeking to manipulate others for our self-interests. We also seek to force our own wills upon people and events. In doing all of this we continue to cultivate our petty interests and feed our growing egos. Only by "putting on the vesture of humility," per Maria Montessori, will we ever be able to live with perspective, insight, and wisdom.

If we do not approach our children with humility and learn from them, we may do more harm than good. Further, it is our responsibility to model for them humility in action, speech and thoughts. We must become humble, and "train" children with our own beingness. Words and admonishments alone will not instruct them. Words are empty and meaningless without our actions and positive role modeling connecting our instruction with our leadership. Children easily know when we are conning them, they see beyond what is visible, they hear past what is being said. We are the ones who are often unaware of when we are conning ourselves.

Helping children cultivate humility puts them on their way to health in their future relationships, school and work life. Lack of humility will only bring children—at various stages of their development—pain, struggle, and disappointment. Therefore, it is up to us as adult role models to become humble ourselves and to model humility for children in their daily lives.

Some Characteristics of Humility

- Seeing each individual's inner beauty; living in beauty, being beautiful.
- Knowing and acknowledging the value of others.

- Respecting the rights of others.
- The willingness to be led and shown.
- Being open and receptive.
- Acknowledging that we don't know all the answers.
- Understanding our own growth.
- Keeping our ideals and our vision.
- Acknowledging our value.
- Sharing mutual values.
- Understanding universal brotherhood.
- Experiencing unity and wholeness.
- Really listening to others.
- Becoming more receptive to the ideas of others.
- Becoming more accepting, understanding, and tolerant.
- Understanding and implementing democratic principles.
- Refraining from judgment, condemnation, and criticism.
- Not imposing our wills or our ideas on others.
- Refraining from arrogance.
- Being less focused on our egos and own needs.
- Becoming more trusting.
- Developing sincerity.
- Developing patience.
- Eliminating our desire to gossip.
- Offering help to others.
- Believing in others, as well as in ourselves.
- Keeping perspective and context in situations.
- Acting with kindness and compassion.

By learning to activate all these qualities, we discover that humility is necessary because it helps create positive human relationships. We see how important these qualities are as they help heal cleavages and problems between people. Exercising humility allows others to be themselves, thus experiencing how the gifts of freedom and acceptance help us and others grow correspondingly in wisdom. We chip away at our defensive egos every time we increase our humility as we are able to examine ourselves honestly, realistically, and with better perspective. We can eliminate arrogance from our lives. Interacting with people who are more skilled than us in various areas helps us develop humility; people who may be more skilled, talented, or successful in areas of work, family, career and service, in handling their own lives and challenges with strength of character. After periods of great struggle, hardship, or conflict, our humility often surfaces. This is also true after we have been helped or "bailed out" by someone or even by life itself. As we develop more humility, we start to sense the presence of a power greater than ourselves, the power and flow of nature, and even the infinite wisdom behind all life.

Activities for Developing Humility

- Seek ways to overcome the ego and its control by learning to observe and distinguish the voice of the ego.
- Search for ways to eliminate the need to control other people, situations, outcomes, or circumstances.
- Begin to trust yourself and the greatness you have been born with.
- Each and every day, wake up and tell yourself that you are a worthwhile person, and that you still have much to learn.

- Maintain the attitude of the learner, whatever your position; parent, leader, manager.
- Continue perfecting your skills of awareness, inner strength, and wisdom.
- Spend a few minutes each day for a week contemplating what is keeping you from being more humble.
- Journal your thoughts and experiences in discovering humility.
- Discuss humility with your children, spouse, family members, friends and associates.
- Recollect occasions in your life where you have been arrogant, insistent, or selfish.
- Contemplate patterns in your behavior that prevent humility from developing.
- Consider areas in your life where you can could improve your humility.
- Study areas where you may be deceiving yourself in forms of self-aggrandizement.

Exploring Humility with Children

- Talk with the child about how they feel about themselves.
- Find out how they feel about various people in their lives.
- Ask the child what they feel if another child says they are superior.
- Ask the child how they would like to be treated by others.
- Help the child discover his ideals.
- Ask the child if he knows other children who pretend to be better than they are.
- Help the child develop self-esteem.
- Ascertain if the child feels inferior or superior to others.

- Discuss what a wholesome perspective on life looks like to a healthy person.
- Support the child in learning and practicing kindness and forgiveness.
- Help the child find acceptance and tolerance of difficult events in school or home, while at the same time encouraging solution-based behaviors.
- Show the child how to become excellent observers of their own bodies, emotions, and minds.
- Help the child learn to observe their social interactions and their motives at home and in school with the goal of seeing wholesome ways to react to the various vicissitudes that come and go.
- Discuss with the child the effects of judging oneself or others.
- Encourage sincerity in the child's actions, speech and thoughts.
- Help the child develop gratitude, to be grateful for all the material and immaterial good things in their lives; their families and friends, food, clothing, and shelter, even the very air we breathe, the sunshine, and all of our planet.
- Motivate the child to help others where feasible.
- Discuss how we are ultimately the custodians of everything in our lives—near and far—and that means we have the responsibility to help others where and when feasible.
- Do charity work together with the child.

These interactive discussions, explorations and activities help foster in the child a humble but powerful sense of belonging to the whole of life. By helping to give our children these perspectives, we encourage a feeling of confidence within the child while at the same time teaching that we all are part of the whole, no part being more important than another part. We breed a healthy humility by teaching forgiveness, joy and life skills.

We inculcate a loving and positive environment at home, work, school, and in the greater society by understanding our role and the roles of others. In challenging situations, as varied as one child yanking away their toy, sibling rivalry, or even when confronted by divorce or death, the child who understands and practices humility gains a calmness derived from understanding context behind phenomena.

As we grow in our own life skills of tolerance, patience, and acceptance, we role-model humility for our children. This will give them the added impetus to become accepting, themselves. As the old adage goes, "Children live what they learn." Our integrated sense of belonging is innately felt by our children. They identify with what they observe. The child develops gratitude—for their lives, families, schools, friends, parents, possessions and the environment—that depends on a sense of humility at the deepest levels. The lifelong values of ethics and personal responsibility arise naturally from this gratitude, helping our children make healthier decisions and choices. And then, even joy itself can arise! Along the way, we remind ourselves and our children that humility, like all the virtues, develops over time and at an individual's own pace. By acknowledging this wonderful path, the process of finding our truest purpose and fulfillment starts to manifest.

Chapter 16
Harmlessness

> Through greater suffering and service, he purifies his emotional nature and expresses only love, blessings and compassion to all living beings. The virtue of harmlessness dominates his heart, and he strives to live a life of helpful service for all humanity.
> – Torkom Saraydarian
> *Christ, The Avatar of Sacrificial Love*, p. 54

> Harmlessness is a great treasure.
> – Torkom Saraydarian *Spring of Prosperity*, p. 62

To be harmless means that we do not create obstacles and hindrances on the path of another. It means we do not create conflicts. We do not bring harm or problems into the lives of others. This sounds very simple, and yet it is one of our greatest challenges.

To be harmless means that we consider the effects of our words and deeds in the light of responsibility. For example, when we make a decision, we consider what effects it will have upon the people directly involved, upon ourselves, as well as on those people indirectly involved such as friends, neighbors, and business associates. When we are harmless, we are anticipating the potential results of our behavior. We are being considerate of what others' needs might be, and what we might do to support these. We act supportively. We think supportively. Further, we squelch within ourselves those behaviors which might take from others, which might hurt them deliberately or inadvertently. We become committed to serving the greater good, or the needs of all those involved. This is the basis of the win-win philosophy.

Harmlessness breeds trust and compatibility in relationships. It allows us to trust each other. We trust others to help and love us, rather than undermining us. We begin to experience the fact that we are all on the same side—the side of life, health, integrity, beauty, goodness, and truth.

The use of harmlessness in our daily lives enables us to be calm, supportive, and self-reliant. We begin to feel the glow of accomplishment because we are living and acting in alignment with our deepest values. When we really live according to our values, we feel joy. In an atmosphere of harmlessness, love blooms and expands.

Imagine the far-reaching implications of harmlessness as applied to the lives of children. Children need harmlessness. In living and working with them, we come to know their hearts. In the hearts of all children—in fact, in the hearts of all people—is the value of harmlessness. We all want to be loved, cared for, protected, and supported by life. This urge in and of itself indicates our yearning for our innate harmlessness to be recognized.

Harmlessness protects life. It stands for beauty and love. It is benevolent. For example, harmlessness encourages us to practice forgiveness and giving in our relationships. It urges us to allow others their idiosyncrasies and differences. Harmlessness rests upon the foundation of our self-awareness, and our inward greatness. The harmless ones are in touch with the uniqueness within themselves. They are aware of the untapped potential within, and are stable, mature people. From this foundation, they can view the positive manifestations of their harmlessness.

Harmlessness expresses itself in a love of life, and responsibility for life—a deep responsibility. It also loves nature and animals, and seeks to protect them. It is open to the beauty in others, and in life. Harmlessness gives, rather than takes. It is compassionate. It serves others. For example, when a non-poisonous, harmless spider is in our house, we kindly take it outdoors in order to help it find a new home. When a cat is lost, we take steps to help find its owner. When a rose bush is uprooted by a storm, we lovingly replant it.

With people, harmlessness expresses itself in a deep consideration of others. We become ultra-sensitive to others, anticipating their needs and wants. We can meet our own needs appropriately in another time slot, in order to help the ones we love in in a harmless way. This is service. This is givingness. It is a form of sacrificial love in action. When we are harmless, we speak words which promote life and good relationships. We become very aware of the issues and concepts which evoke pain in others. Thus, we deliberately steer away from using harsh or unkind words. We become conscious of every word we speak, in order to support the other, and not wound them.

This does not mean that we deny our feelings or hide them. We must be honest. Honesty is harmlessness, too. Our motives must be pure. When we are speaking our minds, do we want to secretly hurt the other? Are we subtly taking revenge? Are we speaking with hidden anger? Are we unforgiving of something long past? Or, are we sincerely wanting to bring resolve and harmony into a situation? These are some of the questions we can ask ourselves as we practice the virtue of harmlessness.

Modeling harmlessness for children may be one of the greatest gifts we can give to them. Children are deluged early on with TV, videos, movies and information which depict just the opposite of harmlessness i.e., violence, competitiveness, fear. Some pop and rock, and hip-hop music demonstrate negative messages. It is easy to carelessly or deliberately harm another person with our thoughts, words, imaginations, and actions. It is more challenging to extend love and joy to them. We are responsible to model and teach our children that the choice is up to us. When we do not meet our responsibilities to others in daily life, we consciously or inadvertently cause harm. We often do not realize how interdependent we are with one another. When we do something or neglect doing it, this has an impact on many lives. We have responsibilities to one another; to love and support each other, to give of our best selves and behave harmlessly toward others.

Children are most sensitive even to casually harmful words, or even a harmful look. Early on they build defenses. We need to show them that embracing our original harmlessness is OK, while still navigating skillfully through harmful environments. Considering our innate harmlessness and its beneficial applications to our life and the lives of our children will change the course of any individual trying to steer themselves away from cynicism, despair or pessimism. Let's continue to ponder, teach and activate harmlessness for the general good of our communities and our international community.

Chapter 17
Forgiveness

> The purpose of forgiveness is threefold:
> a) To create right human relations...
> b) To restore the integrity and honesty of people
> c) To not continue adding to (our) debts...
>
> Grace in its essence is the principle of forgiveness... Only with proper forgiveness can we bring transformation to others, helping them move forward on their paths.
>
> The moment of confession and forgiveness is a sacred moment, and one can be spiritually born again in such moments.
>
> – Torkom Saraydarian
> *Challenge for Discipleship*, p. 464-5

Forgiveness is the key to liberating ourselves and others. Forgiveness sets us free. Forgiveness allows the energies of love and joy to flow freely. When we hold back and do not forgive, we block the flow of love in our lives and in our expressions. Blocked love is the cause of many of our physical and psychological problems. Forgiveness is the first step to set ourselves back on course.

Forgiveness enables us to go forward. It enables us to feel and express love once again. We overcome the limitations and obstacles which were holding us back. Further, we release others to move on, toward their greatest good. We enable things to be resolved in a given situation. This principle of forgiveness applies to individuals as well as groups; to coworkers as well as neighbors, to marriages as well as families, businesses and nations.

With forgiveness, we open the channels for good health to be restored in our relationships. We know that resentment and stored anger eat away at our bodies and our positive mental health. For these reasons, we owe it to ourselves to let go of these stored emotions. When we release them, we will experience dramatically positive results in our lives.

How does forgiveness allow us to experience these goodies? By allowing us to release and let go of those situations which have been holding us back. Forgiveness is a tool for rectifying the situations in our lives that have not worked, or are still holding us back from real progress.

While it may not be immediately obvious to us, our stored anger, and other negative emotions, are preventing us in some ways from moving forward in our lives. What does this mean? It means that while we may have a plan, a goal or a vision of success, we may never quite allow ourselves to achieve it. We may dream of writing that great book. We may dream of starting that project. We may see ourselves as the president of our company. These may be our dreams and visions, and we may sincerely seek them.

Yet, how many of us actually achieve our dreams? How many of us succeed? If we continue to delude ourselves by thinking that our dreams build themselves, we are in for a rude awakening. Of course, we need many things to succeed: Perseverance, commitment, honesty, integrity, purity of motive and heart, just to name a few.

We must not overlook the value of forgiveness in our success picture. We may be so filled with hostility and resentment, even if unknowingly, that we constantly sabotage ourselves. This means that, on some level, we do not allow ourselves to succeed. We live by the effects of our guilt, our rage, our jealousy, our malice. Forgiveness is our only way out. It is our balm. It is our only road to victory. It is our survival. The forgiveness we are talking about is a function of both our own hearts and minds. It is something that goes on within us. It is a transformation.

Forgiveness allows relationships and past wounds to be healed. It also opens the way for us to make progress in our lives. Very often, we hold onto painful memories and carry guilt about events long past. Forgiveness throws this guilt out, allowing love, tolerance, and relief to take over. With relief comes release. Release brings freedom and this release can lead us into new areas of healthy challenge and consequent success in our lives.

Some schools of thought even say that the practice of forgiveness actually paves the way for greater prosperity and abundance in our lives. This would make sense when we consider that by forgiving, we are actually creating an opening in our lives. We are letting go of something. This letting go creates an opening. These openings pave the way for new opportunities to come to us, such as finding a new job, a new relationship, new friendships, or new business opportunities.

Whether this approach can be argued to be true or not, we want to forgive. We want to forgive because forgiveness has real value for our lives. Forgiveness is a just and ethical thing to do. We also like to be forgiven by others for the injustices or harm we may have caused them. When others forgive us, we too are released. This is a two-way occurrence. Everyone involved in the forgiveness process reaps many rewards. These rewards are demonstrated in the form of renewed peace of mind, better health, joy, and courage. Striving and gratitude can grow within us as we forgive and are forgiven.

How does this effect the lives of children? Children living with resentful adults will suffer. It is not possible for adults to be unhappy and secretly resentful, and for children to be unaffected by this. Even when our anger and resentment are slight, there will be distraction and negativity in a child's environment. And children can even become acclimated to negativities. When this happens, they subconsciously come to expect a painful life. If suppressed anger or resentment are modeled for them, they come to expect these forms of behaviors within themselves and others. Yet, when parents express forgiveness, children also learn the importance of forgiveness. When children witness acts of forgiveness and pardon in the household, they in turn learn to do this as well.

Children have in store for them a life of "tests" on the playgrounds of life. Children will face many experiences which will require that they forgive and love, or harbor resentment, and become entrapped in the chains of their egos. We owe it to them to teach and practice forgiveness. We must serve them while they are in our care. We must relay to them the power in forgiveness, the power in love, the power in gentleness.

There is a great nobility in forgiveness. This is attested to by most of us who have been forgiven. Nobility may be at the heart of all healthy, enduring relationships. Nobility is defined as the quality of being exalted in character, ideals or conduct. Interpersonal relating requires the very greatest from us. To rise to these occasions, we must pull the virtue of nobility from within ourselves. This is available to us, especially when we are open to giving and serving, and are motivated by love.

It is interesting to note that the other person does not even have to be present for us to make this attitudinal shift of forgiveness within ourselves. When the forgiven person is present, it adds another healthy dynamic; that is, the opportunity for authentic exchange and a mutual fresh start. Whether the other person is available for us to forgive them in person or not, we must make the effort. We must do it. And further, we must demonstrate all this to the children who have been entrusted to us for they are watching our every move!

Notes on Forgiveness

Forgiveness means:
- Wiping the slate clean.
- Not harboring our resentments.
- Releasing grievances.
- Letting go of resentments.
- Moving on to better things.
- Respecting ourselves and others.
- Reconciliation.
- Resolving conflict.
- Release of the past.
- Giving others the benefit of the doubt.
- Admitting our own follies, weaknesses and habitual behaviors.
- Seeing beyond the surface of events to the true cause.
- Seeing and enacting solutions.

- Acknowledging our minor limitations and setbacks.
- Understanding the continuity of life experience.
- Allowing our innate good to emerge.
- Making room for success.
- Being of service to others.
- Allowing Grace to appear.

In the *New Testament*, we hear Christ saying words to this effect: "Do not let the sun set upon your anger." This is a clear appeal for forgiveness, even daily forgiveness. Forgiveness is needed whenever conflicts arise. We could say that conflicts are an invitation for forgiveness.

We must relay to children the power in forgiveness, the power in love, the power in gentleness. We can teach and model that forgiveness is an attitude, even a position. We can teach that forgiveness first occurs in the heart, yet it is executed as a feeling, a mental state, and an attitude.

Forgiveness Workbook

1. Take some time with a journal or notebook to list every experience and person in your life with whom you are still holding negative energy or negative memories. This can be a list of everything from a sad day in kindergarten when you felt hurt by your best friend to an item-by-item account of your divorce, and any unfinished business you are still holding within yourself. Take time and make this list really comprehensive.

List all the unfinished business you can recall. List the worst to the worst. This list is so important that you may want to keep a running list of negative events, as they occur to you during the time period when you are working on the list.

2. With each event you wish to heal, take time to sit comfortably in a quiet, relaxed room, and do the following activities:

   a. Recall the event. Picture the event and those involved. See yourself. How old are you? What are you doing? How are you feeling? Note any sounds, aromas, words exchanged.
   b. Resolve within yourself to let your negative feelings and memories go, to release them. You may still be getting something out of holding onto them. This is called a payoff. To forgive and be released from the chains of these negative memories, you must be willing to really let go of this payoff, once and for all. You may encounter some resistance to fully letting go. That's fine. If so, journal further about this resistance.
   c. To continue, close your eyes and picture a single event you are ready to let go of today. Choose the one you want to work on at this time. Picture the event the way you recall it. See how you reacted. See the ways others acted, and what you did not like about the event. You can see the situation from your own viewpoint. Then, as much as possible, see the event from the other's viewpoint. It may help for you to relate out loud (eyes open or closed) your side of the story.
   d. Next, and very important, speak out loud as if you were the other person talking to you. Speak or think of the words this person wanted to say to you at the time. Speak as if you were the other person, and say why you

did what you did, thought what you thought, felt what you felt.
e. Now, mentally send forgiveness and love to all those involved. Send joy, beauty and goodness. Feel compassion for the event. Feel compassion for yourself and all those involved. And now, make the commitment to forgive and love this person, and to reconcile. Make the commitment to give up your revenge, malice and pride. Release the need to be right. Release blame. At this time, do everything you can to feel forgiveness and love. With forgiveness, be bighearted to the one who wronged you!
f. Now, picturing the event again, reframe this event. This is done by picturing the entire event as you wished it would have been. What you are doing here is undoing the negative event, and replacing it with a positive outcome. For example, if you were in an argument with someone and you blew up, see yourself in the situation as if it never breaks into an argument. See the two of you resolving the conflict peacefully and appropriately, in the spirit of "win-win." Feel how good it feels to be more in control of your emotional responses. Experience the joy of an event which worked out.
g. Continue to send forgiveness and love to the people involved in these negative events. See yourself forgiving them. See yourself extending goodwill and cooperation to them. Believe within yourself that forgiveness has been achieved. Become committed to creating forgiveness in all your experiences: past, present and

future. This is the result of a positive mental attitude and a decision on your part.

h. Now, write about these negative events in a positive way. Take one event and write directly to the person about how you forgive them. Example: "Dear John, even though you did not pay child support on time, I am glad to forgive you. It's all right that your payments were late. It's all right that you were hostile to me. I know that I did many things to egg you on then. It's forgiven. Let's wipe the slate clean."

Statements to support your forgiveness process are suggested below. These are a beginning. Create your own to fit your needs and experiences:

a. Dear _____, I completely forgive you. Everything is cleared up between us now and forever.

b. Dear ____, I fully forgive you. I forgive you with joy. I forgive you with love. Everything is cleared up between us, and our slate is clean."

c. Dear _____, I release you. I forgive you. I release you and the situation to its highest good. I forgive the past and our difficulties. All is well between us, and I feel joy. I love you.

d. Dear _____, I forgive you. I release you with joy and with love. I am open to the expanded good that the universe now brings us.

e. Dear _____, I release this situation and all involved to their perfect outworking. Our slate is clean.

f. Dear _____, I fully and freely forgive all that has offended me. I accept a healing in this situation now. With love and joy, I embrace life. I have much to rejoice in and much to look forward to.

This is a sampling. You get the idea. Use these daily in the beginning and as you feel appropriate. Using the various techniques and attitudes you are developing, practice daily forgiveness as events arise. Your mental health and well-being are more important than holding onto games of who was right and who was wrong. Forget it. In your heart, embrace the person who hurt you or offended you as your dear friend. Send this person love. Feel it. Find joy in this. Further, feel good about yourself for taking this step.

In your journal, you may want to jot down how you begin to feel about yourself now. In the next few weeks, your journaling may be directly related to your taking these positive steps to forgive others, to forgive the past and to move on. You may need to picture this many times before you accept it, or before your subconscious mind accepts it. You get the idea. This can be done with every item on your list. Don't wait any longer to take these steps in the forgiveness process of healing.

Chapter 18
Respect

Not so many people know what they essentially are. They think they are equal to their body, possessions, certificates, positions, knowledge, or deeds. And because all these are not solid measures, during life and its many problems they become confused about themselves and lose respect for themselves.

If you speak with certain people who are leaning on external values and things to evaluate themselves, they will very sincerely say that they have no respect for themselves, although they demand respect from others.

Once a person begins to realize what they are in their essence, they begin to live a respectful life. He never thinks, speaks, or acts in ugly ways to lose his own (self-respect). A self-respectful person not only respects himself, but they also respect others. They try not to be disrespectful to others, and they evoke from them a mutual respect. Such a person has no jealousy. Whenever someone else is respected, they feel they are respected, too. Whoever respects them, they feel that person respects themself. They always try to live in a way that evokes respect from others. A self- respectful person evokes respect because of their achievements of service, sacrifice, and heroism.

– Torkom Saraydarian
Challenge for Discipleship, pp. 214-15

Everyone wants respect. Everyone knows respect is appropriate for themselves, for others and for life. Talking about respect is socially acceptable. Yet, how many of us constantly respect others in our homes, neighborhoods, workplaces, or society? Our world pays lip service to the term respect, and this is everywhere evident: in the separatism of groups, religions, colleges, private clubs, political parties, and nations. We need a simple reminder of the purpose, quest and results of respect—wherever we might apply it—at home, at school, and in daily life. Many books have been written on the subject but have we missed something?

The Message of Respect

Of course, respect is something that we all crave in both theory and reality. For the child, in particular, the reality of conveyed respect has a very special message. Being shown respect tells the child they have worth, that they are valuable. The child's very existence should be enough to grant them respect in an adult's eyes and in the child's world at large. The child's actions, feelings, aspirations, words and thoughts deserve respect. The child's ideals and aspirations for their future are worthy of respect, whatever they say they want to be when they grow up. Have we missed this message of respect with our children?

Expressing Respect

We express respect to the child by giving them our full and sincere attention, by listening actively to their needs, spoken and unspoken, and in responding to the child by meeting those needs as fully as possible. We adults must realize that it is within our capacity to take action to support the child through the element of respect. Children certainly learn from their parents, teachers, peers, media, and place of worship (or not). They take the gleaned information and, in a sense, then they teach themselves how to cope in an unfamiliar world. The child's development and maturity unfolds from a special place within the child. We can support the direction of the child's life that is ever evolving with respect and even in awe of the process. We observe how the child participates in the flow of life that is guiding all of us, trusting the process through the power of respect.

This is the essence of respect. Maria Montessori spoke of trusting the child; that is, the child's inner powers and unfoldment, the unique powers that she said guide the child to a radiant future. Isn't this the pulse of life, that same essence that is guiding us all? By trusting life, we activate the pulse of respect. By respecting the child, we demonstrate that trust for the child to develop to the best of their abilities.

On all levels, we have the opportunity to respect the child physically, emotionally, mentally, ethically and spiritually. We recognize the child's uniqueness as a being in their own right. At the same time, we must recognize those tendencies in ourselves which inhibit the child or squelch their instincts, or force them to adopt our own standards or our own aspirations for their future. Respect reminds us to allow the child to name their own vision, the vision that is innately coded within them. Therefore, let us always remember the trust we have developed within ourselves that leads to respect for the child and their own process.

Patience as Respect

Respect can also manifest in us as patience. We can watch the child from near and far and remember to exercise patience through their long journey to maturity. We may not understand all of the impulses in the child, nor all of their behaviors. But have we done our own homework to understand our innermost impulses or manifested behaviors? We should remember that we are all explorers, just beginning to find what is real within ourselves and in the world around us. We patiently discover universal and personal truths. We learn to discern what is pretense, illusionary and impermanent. By observing and respecting our own processes, we support exploration and do not degrade it. With that same patience we watch the child, respectfully aiding them to become the magnificent being the child is at the moment and as they evolve to maturity. Respect is part of the child's heritage, is it not?

Self-Respect

In an atmosphere of respect, the child can thrive, and self-respect, esteem, and confidence grows. Respect for the world around develops from self-respect, helping to create harmony and better human relations within the child's environments; school, home, eventually in mating, in the workplace, and the greater community, local and international. With the conscious respect we provide for our child, we help to develop that all important self-respect in them. Starting with self-respect, we are truly preparing the child for life in an atmosphere where the values we hold dear are those that we express, demonstrate and use to help uplift all of mankind.

Respect Activities

Find some time to sit and think about your interaction with your child this week in relation to respect. Think about your words, thoughts, feelings, actions, your attitudes concerning respect.

Begin to write in your journal about your responses to the following questions:

1. Was I respectful? How? When? When did I stop, and why?
2. What circumstances seem to promote my being respectful, and what circumstances seem to prevent it?
3. How do I feel when I am disrespectful? How does the rest of the family feel?
4. What are the consequences of my acting disrespectfully?
5. What would I like to do about these consequences, and the feelings and reactions of my family?
6. How can I find additional ways to be respectful?
7. Activity for your creative imagination:

Find a quiet place, close your eyes and relax. Take a few deep breaths, and put a smile on your face.

Now picture yourself going through the day, or in certain situations, acting respectfully. You may even picture those situations where you are especially tempted to be disrespectful. See yourself conquering this temptation, and victorious in behaving respectfully toward yourself, your child, family, friends, business associates and even strangers. These types of visioning exercises will start to manifest in reality the greater qualities of respect that you are seeking to express and act on for your sake, the child's sake and for the sake of those you meet in your daily life.

Chapter 19
Joy

> Spread the news of joy, spread the ideas of one humanity, spread the ideas of brotherhood of angels and men! Sing, the sons of men are one; I am one with them. Let vision come and insight. Let the future stand revealed. Let inner union demonstrate, outer cleavages be gone!
>
> Sing this song through your thoughts, through your writings, through your feelings, actions and relations. Let people hear you... Tell them the dawn is just minutes away.
>
> Give them joy, as only in joy is the vision understood and the labor carried on. Rejoice!"
>
> – Torkom Saraydarian
> *The Legend of Shambala*, pp. 81-2

A joyful home is harmonious. It is a pleasant place to be, an uplifting place to be. Joy cultivates love in the home. A joyful family is a happy place in which to live together. Children thrive in an atmosphere of joy, love, and beauty. When we begin to raise our children with joy and in joy, so that they are exposed to joy, we will see the budding of a healthier generation.

Joyful people create life wherever they are. Their presence alone is enough to manifest joy in the environment. A joyful person radiates warmth, charisma and magnetism. They infect everything around them with a love for living, a zest for life. Joy manifests enthusiasm. Joy bridges the hearts of people, enabling them to understand one another more fully. It frees them to be themselves because joy demonstrates both trust and acceptance. All of these qualities help create healthy human relationships. And, this is what children need at home and at school.

Joy is a great tonic for families. We all need joy; children do, parents and teachers need joy. Joy is magnetic, healing, and beautiful. Joy charges us with kindness, love and optimism. Joy is the great tonic for our health and vitality. Joy uplifts everything it touches. In an atmosphere of joy, people become relaxed as well as charged with happy energy. Therefore, joy is a healthy virtue to cultivate in our daily lives. Children especially benefit from joy through the joy of their parents, relatives, teachers, and friends. Children absorb the energies or the essence of their environment. Thus, children exposed to joy become joyful.

Joy is not the same as happiness. It is an energy, an attitude, a mindset, an approach to life. Joy can be present despite the most difficult conditions. Our happiness is usually the result of our environment or conditions. Our happiness is usually subject to the conditions of daily life. But joy is beyond all these phenomena. Joy is perhaps more spiritual. It is not the victim of events and it is not squelched by obstacles. It is said that our joy grows during crises, while happiness may disappear. If this is so, we can expose our children to joy, no matter what life circumstances bring us. We can give our children great doses of joy, even if we are undergoing a family crisis. We can model for them an attitude of joy, engendering hope and optimism. We can model for them qualities that are life-enhancing.

We can train ourselves to overcome some of our habitual negativity by being joyful and practicing joy. We can train ourselves to become optimists, forward-thinkers who can reach for the beauty and the lessons underlying all experiences.

Qualities of Joy

- Joy is an energy expressing love and kindness.
- Joy demonstrates goodwill in action.
- Joy and love go together.
- Joy is the Elixir of the Gods.
- Joy is sacred.
- Joy gives a special radiance to people.
- Joy is contagious.
- Joy is an expression of positive, magnetic, and charged energy.
- Joy is vital, vibrant, life-giving, life-enhancing.
- Joy is magnetism.
- Joy is delight.
- Joy is the enthusiasm of the spirit translated into being.
- Joy is the vibration of the soul extended into daily life.
- Joy is aliveness.
- Joy is an intensity animating our best acts.
- Joy is the fire and light in our eyes.
- Joy is the fire of love and the will to love.
- Joy is the fire of the spirit.
- Joy is man's link with the higher kingdoms.
- Joy is the fire striving with love.
- Joy is the fire of enthusiasm and commitment to our best work.
- Joy is openness to oneself and others, adults and children.
- Joy is giving and being generous.

- Joy is reaching out to others and to the world.
- Joy is self-sacrifice, without expectation of recognition or return.
- Joy is radiance, vitality, overflowing energy.
- Joy is being ever-hopeful.
- Joy is being totally present in any given situation.
- Joy is friendliness.
- Joy is autonomous and yet always interconnected.
- Joy is an inner sense of greatness which is not egotistical.
- Joy is inner contentment, serenity.

The Different Forms of Joy

- Joy takes the form of extending ourselves into life's adventures.
- Joy forms relationships with people through intimacy, dignity and integrity.
- Joy forms the sparkle in our eyes.
- Joy is perceived in the form of energy.
- Joy is formed from the pulse of life.
- Joy is a form of special wisdom.
- Joy activates as a form of our love.
- Joy is perceived as the form of refinement in our nature.
- Joy is formed when we work at something we believe in.
- Joy forms our persistence and perseverance.
- Joy is the best form of initiative-taking.
- Joy forms the continuation of our good projects.
- Joy informs us in aliveness.
- Joy is formed from inner enthusiasm outward.
- Joy is formed as kindness and receptivity.

- Joy is the form of creativity.
- Joy forms from inspiration.
- Joy reveals itself in forms of revelations.
- Joy informs visions and insight.
- Joy manifests in form on the quest for true beauty.
- Joy forms as our future.
- Joy comes in the form of optimism and hope,
- Joy forms from our attitudes, behavior, words, thoughts, feelings, actions.
- Joy forms more joy.

The Effects of Joy

- Positive human relationships.
- Positive family life and family environments.
- Clearer thinking.
- Vibrant health.
- More positive mental attitudes.
- Greater focus and direction in our lives and work.
- Confidence.
- Self-trust.
- Commitment to honesty and truth.
- Optimal conditions in which a child can develop.
- Favorable environments for children to develop self-esteem, self-trust, and confidence.
- Beauty of human relationships.
- Trust and intimacy.
- Friendship.

Qualities of Joy

- Openness.

- Giving.
- Generosity.
- Reaching out to others and to the world.
- Self-sacrifice, without expectation of recognition or return.
- Radiance.
- Vitality.
- Overflowing energy.
- Hope
- Giving one's full attention; being totally present in a situation.
- Friendliness.
- Autonomy.
- Serenity.
- Inner Contentment.
- An inner sense of greatness which is not egotistical.

Purposes of Joy

- Joy brings love into our lives.
- Joy manifests love, kindness, freedom, beauty, generosity.
- Joy helps people during crises and challenging situations.
- Joy bridges our physical selves to our spiritual nature.
- Joy manifests the beauty of the higher realm's states.
- Joy demonstrates there is more than our material perceptions.
- Joy allows a fiery love and enthusiasm to achieve all in life.
- Joy propels us happily into our future.

- Joy provokes transformation in ourselves and others.
- Joy points the way to successful human relationships.
- Joy gives children a vision of the greatness within themselves.
- Joy brings inspiration to children to lead great lives.
- Joy purifies our hearts and motives.
- Joy reveals to children the beauty within adults.

Sources of Joy

- Joy that is extended to us from others.
- Joy from a happy home, school and social environment.
- Joy from our children, and our spouse or partner.
- Joy from inspiring our children and others.
- Joy from the release of expectations.
- Joy from remaining strong and serene despite painful events of life.
- Joy from knowing that one is bigger than circumstances or conditions.
- Joy from knowing that our attitudes determine the way we experience life.
- Joy from realizing that we are responsible for our lives.
- Joy from commitment to our plans, vision, dreams, and to ones we love.
- Joy from actions performed in the spirit of sacrifice.
- Joy from performing actions in the spirit of unconditional giving.
- Joy from doing all we can for those we love.
- Joy from doing something larger than our perceived capacities.
- Joy from pledging ourselves to serve others.

- Joy from experiencing our own creativity.
- Joy from giving joy to others.

Obstacles to Joy (and Love)

Writer Torkom Saraydarian, who has done years of studies on joy and love, details their characteristics in his books. He also lists twelve main obstacles to our joy and love. He writes, "If you conquer these obstacles, your joy and love will increase."

Obstacle 1: Pressure.

Anytime you exercise pressure on others, or seek to force your will upon the will of others, love and joy weaken and eventually disappear. Joy and love increase only in a state of freedom.

Obstacle 2: Jealousy.

Jealousy saps the energy of joy and love. Jealousy wants to possess and whoever possesses anything eventually loses their joy and love. They lose life. Jealousy prevents growth of joy and love between people.

Obstacle 3: Denial of Freedom to Others.

Such a violation literally extinguishes the flame of your joy and love. Only in freedom does joy increase and love bloom. Let the one you love be free. In their freedom find your joy. Let that person decide, or plan and follow their own conscience, use their own free will. If you keep such an attitude, not only to your closest ones but to all people, you will see the increase of joy and love in your heart. Respect the ideas and the visions of others. Be tolerant and help them respect your ideas and visions too. If your ideas and visions are more inclusive, you will increase your joy and love.

Obstacle 4: The tendency to misuse people and their belongings.
With such a tendency, joy and love eventually evaporate because the spirit of exploitation rests in your heart.

Obstacle 5: Non-inclusiveness.
Non-inclusiveness is a great enemy of joy and love. Joy and love are like fragrances. They expand and spread. Non-inclusiveness creates barriers and walls within you. Inclusiveness opens the path of expansion. Joy and love cannot be caged. They must flow and expand. Inclusiveness leads to right human relations, to international understanding, to respect, and appreciation.

Non-inclusiveness is self-worship, separation, which eventually breeds aggressiveness, hate, and conflict. Joy and love disappear in an atmosphere of separation. Once they disappear, hate and depression take their place.

Obstacle 6: Unrighteousness (Injustice).
If you are unrighteous in your thoughts, emotional responses and actions you will not have real joy in your heart, and love will never bloom in you. Joy and love increase when you respect the rights of other people. Those people who do not act rightfully to others carry a heavy burden in their conscience, and eventually that burden turns into a pressure, expressing itself through various sicknesses and complications in their lives. A

righteous person has joy and love even if people do not understand them.

Obstacle 7: Ugliness.

Beauty increases joy and love. Ugliness makes them disappear. Your joy and love fade away when you experience an ugly thought, emotion, action, or any ugly expression. Your thoughts are ugly when they are selfish, harmful, criminal, divisive or false. Your emotions are ugly when they are negative, when they lack solemnity. Your actions and expressions are ugly when they are destructive, insulting, belittling, and motivated by self-interest. As one removes ugliness from their surroundings, from their thoughts, emotional reactions and actions, joy fills their heart, and love increases in them. Beauty always shines in joy and love.

Obstacle 9: Insincerity.

No love or joy exists in a heart which has an insincere attitude toward other human beings. Joy and love cannot exist where sincerity is absent. An insincere person eventually finds their joy and love fading away. To have joy and love, one

Obstacle 10: Nosiness.

A nosy person cannot increase their joy and love. The nosy person is always occupied with personality affairs. They criticize and judge. They interfere with the decisions of others, mentally or verbally. They evoke reactions and involvement with the personal lives of others. Love does not like nosiness. Joy does not live where there is imposition of thoughts and manners. Nosiness increases your worries and hurts other people. A nosy person cannot gain their freedom. Often, they are caught in the net of gossip.

Obstacle 11: Criticism.

Criticism creates rejection. Every time you criticize you impose yourself on others. You impose your personality on others. Criticism does not let other people experience and experiment. It does not let them grow and be themselves. Criticism presents and imposes its own molds and wants everyone to be molded by its standards. Thus, it limits the horizons and striving of others. Joy and love cannot grow and expand in an atmosphere of criticism. Joy and love exist for all. When you hurt someone, you hurt your love and your joy.

Obstacle 12: Carelessness and Pride.

The two go together. Love cares. Joy communicates and identifies with others, and with the success and achievements of others. Carelessness leads one to irresponsibility. Where the sense of responsibility does not exist, there is no conscious love and real joy, the two great pillars of light which lead people toward universality and toward the highest values of life.

– Torkom Saraydarian,
The Flame of Beauty, Culture, Love, Joy
pp. 203-206

Activities to Cultivate Joy

1. Joy begins with a certain frame of mind, an attitude. Consider what mental state of mind you would need to cultivate more joy in your life, or what kind of attitudinal change would be required for you to feel more joyful.
2. After you have located the attitudes you would need to change to become joyful, design a way to change them, to facilitate this joy. Consider the positive outcomes in your personal and family life which would result from your joy and vitality. How do you feel about your new attitudes? How much do you want to implement and live with these positive changes? Are you willing to make the commitments and even the sacrifices necessary to facilitate a more joyful you?
3. How can you actualize the changes you have conceptualized? How will you draw on the strength of purpose to actualize these changes?
4. Ask what you can do to surround yourself, your household and your school with beauty. Make your environment radiate beauty with flowers, plants, art or even lighting. Beauty will promote joy.
5. Expose yourself and your family to positive cultural activities both at home and outside the home.
6. Grasp on to positive media news and events, such as new innovations that help solve local and international problems. Share such news with your children and family. Read and share uplifting stories and books which detail heroic deeds done by ordinary people that help humanity.
7. Sing more often. Sing with your children, friends and family. Sing happy and inspiring songs. Feel joyful as you

sing energetically and with appreciation for the words and melodies of the songs.
8. Do something needed or do something that is just nice for someone and lets them know you appreciate them. Prepare a special treat for your family or classroom. Give even when you may not be in the mood to give to someone. Stretch yourself, and even give away something precious to someone.
9. Buy your spouse, your children, or your family some special clothes, or even just a cute pair of socks or a funny hat.
10. Speak and act consciously with love towards someone for no particular reason.
11. Think loving thoughts towards someone.
12. George Bernard Shaw said, "There is the true joy of life; to be used by a purpose recognized by yourself as a mighty one." Find joy in serving a community, serving or supporting others.
13. Create a sense of adventure for your children. Speak with joy, even some drama or spice. Accentuate the excitement of experiences such as noting the color of the sky, hearing the songs of birds, feeling the texture of leaves, or watching the beauty of sunset. Help children discover the joy of living, the joy of nature and the joy of life's adventures.
14. Create a family ritual by reciting a poem or a prayer before meals or bedtime. Let the words be inspiring, full of gratitude and meaning.
15. Talk with your spouse or partner and your children about further ways to create joy at home. Have these discussions on a regular basis.

16. Develop a greater value within yourself, more self-esteem for the benefits of joy to emerge, for the life-enhancing qualities of joy to emanate more and more from your life, to those who share your life.

Chapter 20
Sincerity

> Your progress and improvement in life depend on your ability to fight, on your sincerity, and on your wholeheartedness. When you win a "battle," a strange thing will happen. All your enemies and past failures will become your friends because they will be used as experiences and sources of wisdom. You will know better because you learned wisdom by going through many experiences.
>
> – Torkom Saraydarian
> *Challenge for Discipleship*, p. 94

> Simplicity inspires sincerity.
>
> – Torkom Saraydarian
> *The Psyche and Psychism*, p. 894

Sincerity is the quality of being free from pretense, deceit, and hypocrisy. Sincerity mostly has to do with our motives. When we approach people and situations with a pure heart and pure motives, we feel clean and events seem to flow. Sincerity in our motives, words and behavior, helps to build relationships. It nourishes our experiences with others, especially with the significant people in our lives. Our sincerity also nourishes those with whom we relate, and it nourishes their experiences.

We can sense when we are faking it and being insincere. If we are open enough, we know when others are being insincere with us. Children are given a valuable gift when we give them the gift of our sincerity. Children, especially, are experts at perceiving insincerity. Very few people can get by their eagle eyes and refined senses. Children tend to recognize a con. It is important that we realize how sensitive and attuned to truth they really are. We owe it to them and to ourselves to live up to their need for honesty, integrity, and sincerity. We are either being real and sincere with them, or we are lying. Our level of authenticity with them will either support or sabotage their lives.

Chapter 21
Discipline

Discipline is the beginning of everything.
> *The Leaves of Morya's Garden*, Vol. II, p. 154

A child readily obeys an adult. But when an adult asks him to renounce those instincts that favor his development, he cannot obey. When an adult demands such a sacrifice to his own personal interests, it is like attempting to stop the building of a child's teeth when he is teething. A child's tantrums and rebellions are nothing more than aspects of a vital conflict between his creative impulses and his love for an adult who fails to understand his needs. When a child is disobedient or has a tantrum, an adult should always call to mind the conflict and try to interpret it as a defense of some unknown vital activity necessary for the child's development.
> – Maria Montessori
> *The Secret of Childhood*, p. 104

Discipline is a process of mastery.
> – Torkom Saraydarian
> *Challenge for Discipleship*, p. 336

A child measures justice better than a judge. Wherefore can only the aged and the children be the arbiters of the earth?
Human judgment blunders.
Laws obstruct the entrance.

Learn to judge in the open, beneath the stars. Learn to measure distances with the closed eye. To see the light with the closed eye is granted to each one. But, laziness, ingratitude, ignorance, and brutality are astride your backs.

Blind travelers, how will you attain the justice of children?

Wash away the dust of the habit.

Leaves of Morya's Garden, Vol. I, p. 293

Chapter 22
Simplicity

Simplicity is the ability to let things stand as they are. It is also the revelation of beauty without our interference. It has been said in literature, "Beauty is truth, and truth is beauty." Truth can also be simple, and that can be part of its beauty, a simple beauty.

Young children need a simple environment to get accustomed to life. Yet older children benefit from simplicity to offset the ever-increasing developmental complexity of their lives. Young children, passing through their sensitive periods of growth, must be exposed first to the simple factors around them. They should have walls which are simple and tasteful, colors which will be harmonious for them to live with daily, and adults who will speak to them simply, and explain things simply. The young child's mind does not organize itself well with clutter. It is in its most vital formative stages, and it should be fed a diet of love, beauty, patience, and simplicity.

This means that we must learn to answer children's questions directly, and with compact answers. We must train ourselves to be succinct. This will do much for children, for their growing understandings of life, and their integration with the world around them. Moreover, simplicity will facilitate within the child clearer thinking, greater insight, even compassion, and a more sympathetic point of view. As we train ourselves in the art of simplicity, as our thinking and speech become clearer and simpler, we are better able to lead our children. One potentially confusing habit we adults do is to expose others to our thinking process aloud. We speak while simultaneously thinking through what we really believe about a topic. This sometimes creates confusion in communication and it can muddle our own lives. Put upon young children, unclear thinking and communicating can confuse them unnecessarily.

Simplicity can be applied in every area of our lives with great success. We can cultivate simplicity in our dress and in our children's wardrobes; in our homes and décor, in children's rooms and playrooms, in family and school activities, in our words and writings and in all our actions. We can coach children in simplifying their lives with love and tenderness.

We may just coach them along with simple reasoning, calmly and even with a sense of humor and joy.

Activities to Cultivate Simplicity

1. During pregnancy, early childhood, and throughout the child's young life, make sure the items you surround the child with items that are simple, appealing, and beautiful. Many manufacturers cram toys, clothes and furniture with distorted pictures of animals and cartoons. Often, we find complex designs everywhere; printed onto fabric, sheets, wallpaper, slippers, diapers, drinking cups and plastic dishes. When we infuse the child's environment with simple elements, we are creating an open and welcoming place for resourcefulness, imagination and innovation. Even during pregnancy, we can prepare this type of

environment for the infant. Beauty is key, avoiding distortion. Cartoons are usually distorted.
2. Begin to simplify your own speech on a daily basis. Practice writing a declarative sentence. Then change it around as many times as possible, simplifying it each time you change it while maintaining its original meaning throughout this process. Keep a journal with all the sentences you simplify.
3. Begin to observe yourself and others regarding times when you are wordy, or when you express yourself in a simple way. Note your feelings. Ask whether the conversation could have been just as meaningful if it were simplified? Why do you think we are too wordy? What payoffs and liabilities do you think wordiness brings us?
4. Observe the decor around you: public places like restaurants, offices, department stores, supermarkets. What do you notice?
Visit toy stores with the intention of observing the toys' loud, sometimes abrasive colors and designs. How do you feel when you are in the store? How do you imagine children feel in handling toys with distorted or caricature faces and glaring fluorescent colors? What more simple alternatives can you find, or would you create for children?
5. Seek to develop greater simplicity in all your relationships: with your spouse or partner, with children, relatives, boss, neighbors and co-workers. Observe the effects of relating with more simplicity in your life and in your relationships.

Chapter 23
Diligence

> Diligent and conscientious efforts made on behalf of children will enable us to discover the secret of mankind just as scientific investigations have enabled us to penetrate into so many of the secrets of nature.
> – Maria Montessori
> *The Secret of Childhood*, p. 4

To be diligent is defined as the constant effort to accomplish something; being attentive and persistent in doing anything; pursued with persevering attention, painstaking, industrious, indefatigable, untiring; with persistent exertion of body and mind. What an incredible gift we can give our children by modeling for them the virtue of diligence.

Diligence is responsibility and skill in action. Diligence uses our practical skills in bringing to life our visions and plans. When we work with diligence, we eventually get things done. We accomplish our plans and dreams. We finish what we start. We complete our projects. And we are diligent with a positive attitude, with a giving and caring attitude. We are diligent with love and with a sense of responsibility and striving.

When we work with diligence, we demonstrate that work is love made visible. There is no better way to model a positive attitude toward life and its responsibilities, than to show our children that we do everything with diligence. Giving children this gift will help them internalize the positive values we want them to exhibit during all seasons of their development. Children will learn the essence of responsibility and duty by watching everything we do with diligent qualities of care, concern, striving, and attentiveness.

Cultivating Diligence

Here are some activities you may wish to do to help your child become more diligent. These are questions which may be used as seed thoughts for journaling. They may be used as discussion topics at home, among spouses, friends, neighbors, and coworkers. Or, you may wish to use them as topics to think about.

Diligence Inventory

- What am I doing to help my child learn and follow through on the ground rules at home and in school?
- What am I doing to help my child develop concentration?
- What am I doing to help my child become responsible?
- Do my children know that if they work or play with things that they must also put away those things, clean or take care of them for future use?
- What can I do to enhance their skills in these areas?
- Am I helping my children become consistent in their habits, goals, and daily lives?
- What can I do to aid them in learning consistency?

- What can I do to help my children set goals for themselves, goals that are important to them for a holistic and balanced life?
- How can I help my children learn to make plans and learn organizational skills?
- What can I do to help them learn constructive follow-through?
- How can I encourage my children to gain persistence and perseverance?
- Do I follow through on the ground rules that I am setting out for my children?
- In what ways can I introduce various skills for self-discipline to my children?
- What can I do to help my children monitor their own actions, words, thoughts and feelings?
- How can I teach the necessary steps to self-correction?
- What am I doing to help my children learn the values of effort and exertion?
- What am I doing to instill in my child the love of service, the joy of work?
- How am I helping my child learn to work with attentiveness, accuracy, beauty, and attention to detail?
- How am I helping my child gain respect for their work, and work in general, whether the work is fun or not?
- How can I teach my child the joy of stretching limits, conquering obstacles, multiplying our resourcefulness and abilities?
- Do I practice and demonstrate diligence in my own life? How and when?

Chapter 24
Beauty

> The highest achievement of the human soul is the moment of identification with the principle of beauty. When a certain number of teachers, leaders, and public officials are graduated with the qualifications of beauty, then we will see the dawn of a new life."
> – Torkom Sarydarian
> *The Flame of Beauty, Culture, Love, Joy*, p. 45

The word beauty is defined generally as the quality or aggregate of qualities in a person or thing that gives pleasure to the senses or pleasurably exalts the mind or spirit. When a child lives with beauty in the home, beauty within the family and its relationships and beauty at school, they learn to appreciate the qualities of beauty. Conversely, the lack of beauty, even when expressed in various negative ways creates cleavages on the path to the appreciation and creation of beauty. Any sort of negativity acts as an obstacle to a successful and fulfilling beautiful family life. When a home is filled with human expressions of beauty, then new vistas for children expand to enhance their lives.

Research is being published now on the effects of beauty in the environment; effects on behavior, mood, physical vitality and motivation. The findings reveal that beauty in the environment transforms and uplifts us. Beauty can help make a positive impact on symptoms such as hypertension, depression, and other nervous disorders. Psychologically we know that beauty gives us the sense of freedom. The applications of beauty are universal and unlimited.

> Children must be put in touch with beauty not only in their art classes but they also must be taught how to see beauty, how to enjoy beauty, and how to be beautiful. They must learn to see the beauty in flowers, in great rivers and waterfalls, in all forms of life, and to come in contact with the creative beauty of great artists.
> – Torkom Saraydarian
> *The Flame of Beauty, Culture, Love, Joy*; pp. 16-7

> The true nature of Divinity is expansion, and the result of expansion is Beauty, and the sense of Infinity. This comes to all who do not tolerate limitations of the expression of beauty.
> *Ibid*, p. 79

> Our limitations are what stop us. We must not allow ourselves to be stopped as we strive toward achievement. We may achieve many things in the realms of beauty, contributing these to our families, children, and workplace. "Striving toward beauty leads us to the future."
> *Ibid*, p. 6

Beauty Awareness Activities

Nature

Help your children learn to appreciate nature in all its glory. Note in nature the beauty of water, streams, rivers, lakes, waterfalls, the ocean. Show children the many ways beauty manifests in all these things—through sound, color, the spray of the water, the aromas. Help educate children's very alive senses. The beauty and even the music of the wind and the breeze should be recognized as they pass through your neighborhood, as they pass through the woods. Point out the sounds the wind makes as it sweeps through the trees, bushes, and fields. The beautiful music of the birds at dawn and sunset are listened to with appreciation. The unique, beautiful markings of all the birds are noticed by parents and children. The patterns and formations in which the birds fly, their ways of communicating with each other, viewing their various nesting places attests to the varieties of beauty in nature. Cultivate in children appreciation for the beauty of the mountains, plains, hills, and forests; the beauty of the stars.

Music

Expose children to classical music, symphonies, concerts and choral music at home, school, in the car, through season tickets to children's concerts, and the Symphony. When it comes time to buy gifts for children, helping them develop their own music collection is a wonderful gift. Buy music for them at their age level, and yet do not underestimate their capacity to enjoy more sophisticated music selections. Children have been shown to derive great enjoyment from traditional classics like Mozart, Beethoven, Strauss, and Handel. If children manifest an interest in learning to play a musical instrument, to sing or to dance, do all you can to enable them to study in school and after school with excellent instructors in this quest for artistic beauty.

Voice

Reveal to children the beauty and music of the human voice. Speak in a beautiful manner with them, being articulate and using your vocal tones skillfully. Be aware of the potential beauty in your own voice, and your capacity for using it constructively or destructively.

Visual

Introduce children to beauty in the visual realm by helping them recognize beauty in what they see. Help them find beauty in colors, movements, forms, relationships, proportions, paintings and other art works; including art by the master artists of history, available to be seen in museums and through various media that are available today.

Emotions

Introduce children to the beauty of human emotions such as love, personal and universal, respect, courage, kindness, peacefulness, enthusiasm, joy, tenderness, gratitude, harmlessness, patience, and compassion. All of these wonderful emotions are demonstrated by parents, family and teachers. The dramatic arts are a good place for children to study the panoply of human emotions.

Great Ideas

Great heroes, great leaders and geniuses in any field are those who are inspired by great ideas, by great goals and great visions. This is how cultures evolve into great civilizations. By studying the great works of great writers, thinkers, and creators throughout the ages, children start to grasp the beauty of great ideas.

By being allowed to participate in the discovery of beauty, children become the coworkers of those women, men, and even other children from all times who strove to make the world a better place, a more beautiful place. Through the appreciation of beauty, children will become more well-rounded citizens, prepared to live great lives filled with great creative endeavor in whatever fields they choose as their own. What a lasting and irreplaceable gift we give children when we fill their lives with beauty, showing them how to experience lives that are filled with meaning and purpose.

Inventory on Beauty

For those who are open and ready, Beauty:
- Expands awareness, perspective, and consciousness.
- Inspires new visions.
- Harmonizes unrelated ideas in the mind.
- Brings new revelations.
- Releases energies hitherto untapped within us.
- Evokes joy and love.
- Dispels fear.
- Makes a person inclusive.
- Opens the gates of generosity.
- Awakens greater tolerance.
- Fills us with solemnity.
- Creates healthy human relations.
- Increases goodwill.
- Reveals the sense of Infinity.
- Transforms lives of people.
- Creates efficiency in work.
- Creates goals. Inspires a striving towards betterment in life.

- Creates the sense of responsibility.
- Inspires respect for others.
- Raises consciousness to higher values.
- Creates better health on physical, emotional, and mental levels.
- Motivates healthy human relationships and goodwill.
- Helps to understand harmlessness.
- Gains views of broader and more inclusive social relationships.
- Awakens greater sensitivities.
- Inspires better communications.
- Inspires the spirit of gratitude.

> There is not a phase of human life which cannot be improved by the power of beauty.
> – Torkom Saraydarian
> *The Flame of Beauty, Culture, Love, Joy*; p. 24

Chapter 25
Culture

> Let us welcome those schoolteachers who can find an hour to talk to their pupils about the dignity and responsibility of man, and about the treasures belonging to all peoples.
> – Agni Yoga Society *Brotherhood*, para. 601

> There should be instilled (in children) respect for culture in order that it be understood as a higher distinction. Ancient working-community guilds left testimony of their vitality. One can see how people cultivated their skills toward perfection. They knew how to shield each other and how to guard the dignity of their community. So long as people do not learn to defend the merit of their fellow-workers they will not achieve the happiness of the Common Good.
> – Agni Yoga Society
> *New Era Community*, para. 12

We can define culture as the arts, customs, institutions and other manifestations of human intellectual and spiritual achievement regarded collectively by a nation, a people or other social group.

One of the ways we can expand our children's horizons is to introduce them to culture in order to enrich their worlds and to improve their experiences. We can give our children the whole breadth of our culture and world cultures through the study of human history, science and the arts. The journey of cultural awareness can start very early in the child's development. This doesn't need to cost much money. A few library books, visits to museums, geography lessons with a globe, explanations of various holidays around the world—these are good ways to begin the wonderful journey of culture.

We can play quiet classical music in children's rooms, before naptime, before sleep. Mozart, Handel, Bach, and Palestrina can provide beauty and inspiration.

When we broaden our minds and the minds of our children, we broaden our worlds. We enlarge our caring and concern for others, for the environment and for ourselves. We broaden our hearts. The exploration of culture unites us with others, with the hearts and lives of others, and with their unique traditions.

For our children, we are raising awareness, compassion and empathy via cultural studies and experiences. Children begin to know that others are important too, that other people have lives that are interesting and worthy of value. Culture is the way to learn of life and its diverse forms of celebration. Cultural learning opens up many varieties of life opportunities previously unimagined.

With the very young child, we can give them simple experiences with culture such as artifacts, diverse musical instruments, and non-scary masks. As the child develops, field trips to museums and archeological sites, world music, assorted foreign costumes, can be introduced for study and appreciation.

Resistance to Cultural Explorations

As we know, children oftentimes need to exert their independence by resisting their parents' suggestions, especially in exploring unfamiliar territory. There will be those children who resist going to museums and to the symphony.

This simply presents the adult opportunities for negotiation. Having a family council meeting can be helpful in these cases. Flow with the situation, and remain flexible. Be open and not judgmental.

Helping the child to feel they are making independent decisions, taking risks and understanding consequences are all part of the process to developing personal responsibility. An open and welcoming attitude on your part will help the child lay the foundation to experience freedom, choices, and decision-making. The child will come to experience the results of their decisions and actions, spurring the development of their personal responsibility.

Pointing out the benefits of exploring various cultural activities on terms that appeal to the child helps to afford a positive response. Helping the child understand how their firsthand experiences of cultural exploration will aid them in their own worlds and with their peers, will also assist them in recognizing causes and effects of larger cultural issues in their own lives. We don't want to coerce our children to study culture or to attend cultural events but being patient and explaining the benefits will eventually bear fruit. Maria Montessori famously said, "Follow the child," and we can also put wonderful cultural offerings on the table for them from which to pick and choose their interests.

Readings about Culture

> Culture is the translation and interpretation of beauty. The labor to share beauty is culture. When you have culture, you have a bridge extending from the source of beauty to you. It is this that will transform your life as you strive, labor, and

eventually penetrate into the mysteries of beauty. The door to that beauty is within yourself. Any person who becomes self-actualized, anyone that eventually becomes himself— free from all mechanical influences—radiates beauty. As in the universe, in each human being there is hidden the creative beauty, and self-realization is the process of becoming oneself which is a process of creativity and manifestation of beauty.

– Torkom Saraydarian
The Flame of Beauty, Culture, Love, Joy; p. 60

Culture is transformation, self-actualization. One can be educated, yet not cultured. Education is the collection of facts; culture is transformation of one's nature. Culture cannot be created through knowledge only, but through the transformation of life. Education is our society's way of gaining material things; education is the study of culture. The whole subject of education is civilization and culture. Culture is the manifestation of beauty. Education can learn about culture, but it cannot create it, unless man transforms himself.

Ibid p. 65

Every time we contact true culture, we are energized and revitalized. This is how a sunset or sunrise affects us. That is what a great book or a great painting does for us.

Ibid p. 67

The prime quality of culture is upliftment. True culture leads toward cooperation, unity and synthesis; toward happiness and joy. Culture integrates and brings one together. Culture opens one to greater insights, deeper visions, and a greater willingness to serve and sacrifice for humanity. Culture makes one highly creative.

Ibid p. 68

There is no cultural manifestation without heavy efforts. To bring beauty into expression is not an easy job. It takes courage, daring, striving, and heavy labor. Through culture people come closer to each other. Through culture, the boundaries of races, colors, countries, and religions are eliminated. Culture provides the only language through which races can communicate with each other.

Culture may manifest through the characteristics of individual races or nations, but in its essence, it is universal because the source of culture is beauty. When beauty blooms through all human endeavors, we have culture.

Ibid p. 80

True culture will eliminate from the world the entire trash in which we are living; the crimes, the deceptions, exploitations, hypocrisy, greed, fear, selfishness, and their like. It is very important also that people expose themselves to culture gradually. There are people who run away from beauty or from creative people; the voltage is too much for them. They can develop an antagonism if we force them to contact cultural phenomena. If the capacity of a person's reception is limited then he becomes flooded and feels irritated because he cannot assimilate the beauty. Then he either hates or rejects culture.

Ibid p. 82

There is also the psychological fact that when faced with a great beauty, some people develop an intense fear. This is very interesting because in great beauty a person loses himself.

Exposure to great beauty is like throwing oneself into the ocean; first there is fear, but then once you lose that fear you experience joy and identification with the ocean.

Ibid p. 85

To produce great cultures, a nation or group of highly creative people must have no discord within the system. Only a unified field of energy can create and manifest beauty.

Ibid p. 86

The Effects of Culture

- Culture charges others with an uplifting, regenerating energy which cheers them up, energizes and helps them enjoy life.
- Culture creates right human relations. One stands for and embodies harmony, unity, and understanding.
- Culture breaks separating walls between people, walls made by prejudices, emotions, thoughts, and traditions.
- When the electricity of culture flows through a person, releasing the power of beauty within, it creates unity, and wipes away all the walls of separation existing within that person.
- Culture creates international unity and beauty urging one to cooperate, to share, and even to renounce ugliness.
- Through culture we develop sensitivity to great ideas and new directions.
- Through culture we expand ourselves, becoming more inclusive allowing brotherhood to be achieved through expansion of global awareness.

Enjoy culture as a family. Develop observation skills in yourself and in your children at home and in your classroom. Wherever there is culture, you and your children can observe and appreciate the harmony of nature, the uniqueness of people, the order of society, the flow of simple and complex systems. The beauty of our own calmness and humanity attests to cultural celebration. Our commitment to culture and its abiding beauty gives our new generations a foundation that reward our children and ourselves with a continuing and worthwhile heritage.

Chapter 26
Adaptability

We know that our lives will change once children arrive, but we seldom picture how much. The birth of a child, or the adoption of a child, brings great change into a household. Raising children demands change from us, change in our life-styles, and even our entire approach to life. One of the main skills to develop (and early on in our new caretaker roles) is the skill of adaptability. Adaptability promotes our skills in becoming flexible, having more give and take, adjusting to changing circumstances in the moment, giving up rigidity.

Our skills in these areas reflect our general success in life. To the degree that we have developed these vital skills, we will lead our lives successfully. Further, our level of maturity in some measure reflects our abilities to be responsive, authentic and responsible as conditions continuously change, sometimes in very challenging ways.

A mature person develops the skills to make sound choices. A mature person gives up being overly sensitive, selfish or narrow-minded. A mature person reflects reason and integrates logic with their intuition and instinct. This means that in a mature person both heart and mind are blending into a working unity. When we are operating on these levels, we will become the best parents, grandparents, caregivers, and teachers to our children. We will be the healthiest role models for youth. We will be examples of sanity, beauty and stability to our families and communities. This type of maturity, incorporating the skills of adaptability, builds bridges which create constructive relationships between people, situations, groups, and even nations.

Our ability to be adaptable and flexible births a sincere and intelligent person who lives fully in the stream of life. Demonstrating our adaptability in daily life signals tolerance and openness. We use discernment in the moment, based on our experience and mindfulness, to select the most appropriate choice in a situation. We choose between competing priorities, values or demands. As parents, teachers, caregivers, and ultimately decision-makers, we learn to apply wisdom and guidance in an elastic and pliable manner as our children require this kind of fluidity.

Simultaneously, we must become flexible learners, adaptable to learning from our children's words, emotions and behavior. We must be able to adapt our thinking, pre-conceived notions, and previous experiences in order to change as our children grow and change. When we are open to having our minds and old beliefs changed by our new caretaking experiences, we are giving children a gift that helps them throughout their development. And of course, when we are open to learning through our adaptative skills, we become more educated and wiser, as well as humble.

It is clear that in raising children, we must adapt ourselves to their proclivities. We must adapt ourselves to who our children are and to what they show us. This means that if a child demonstrates musical interest or abilities, we must not impose our wish that they become a doctor. If she is wonderful at math and science, we must not insist she become a ballerina. This kind of acceptance based on our adaptability to present realities gives children the gift of allowing them to become their fully individuated selves. We are empowering our children by being open to the expression of their true greatness. Isn't this what we want?

Maybe yes, and maybe no. We must always look closely at this. Most of us say we want the best for our children. Yet, there are parents who continue to indulge their own unhealthy habits or indulgences rather than spend more on their futures, more on children's current and future needs. Spending more on the latest acquisitions than on music and dance lessons, on extra tutoring, is not an indicator of adaptability to the needs of the child. And yes, there are parents who may even be jealous of their children, not encouraging or supporting their successes, even being abusive. This calls for self-transformation.

Are we competitive with our children, knowingly or unknowingly? Our awareness of conflicting wants in raising children requires the insight, discipline and adaptability to change our attitudes and our hurtful behaviors. Our interest in changing ourselves and upgrading our lives is also related to our levels of adaptability, open-mindedness, and flexibility.

Family life and school hours are never dull, full of challenges. Events frequently occur which test both our judgment and adaptability. Families will always experience circumstances and conditions requiring both wise adaptability and judicious choices. We can approach decision-making as a wonderful challenge to our discriminative abilities. When we are faced with a decision about our family or about our child, we can fret over and create stress in our bodies and minds. Or, we can rejoice over the chance to be resourceful and creative. We can create joy over the opportunity for us to demonstrate greater and more effective levels of parenting. Choices, decisions, and even obstacles can become fertile ground for us to demonstrate our growing flexibility and adaptability to life, and our growing maturity, as parents, grandparents, caregivers, and teachers. This is an aspect of true leadership.

What a great joy it is for us to experience those moments of mastery over challenging situations; of mastery over our own problems and sorrows. What a great joy it is for us to work through challenging situations with our children, and to emerge feeling good about the way we handled these. This all becomes increasingly possible as we grow our flexibility and adaptability muscles, along with developing greater discernment. Our positive experiences in these areas with our children, our families, and in our schools, ultimately serve us and our communities with affirmative outcomes that we can be proud to have ushered in through these challenges.

Chapter 27
Closing Notes on Values, Virtues, and Character Development

> A new era begins when we live a life of higher cooperation, unity, understanding and with a more sensitive response to the creative forces in man and nature.
> – Torkom Saraydarian
> *The Flame of Beauty, Culture, Love, Joy*; p. 90

My hope is that this book has been inspirational and motivational for parents, grandparents, Nannies, educators and child-life professionals. There is no intention to be judgmental, nor to lay guilt. The vision of living ethics for children and the values highlighted here *are simply meant to offer a roadmap for healthy relationships and healthy lives*. Our children, our families, schools, and communities can always study and refine blueprints for more effective and fulfilling relationships.

Some of us are at the beginning of our journeys to acknowledge and employ these values in our lives. Some of us know the materials but maybe are a bit rusty in certain areas. Perhaps the experts who read this material will be stimulated by some new idea not previously considered by them. In any case, our sincere appreciation of these values and their roles in our lives, plus our intention to actualize them are ways we move toward a more ideal world condition than the one we have had to accept traditionally.

We must first want and seek the holistic changes we have been defining and discussing. Then, we must believe that we are the ones who can effect these changes. There exists great strength in numbers. If we entertain doubts about our abilities, these doubts will undermine our effectiveness. To be successful in actualizing these values, we must truly believe we are capable and that we can align and unite with others who seek similar goals for children and our world. Then the journey starts and becomes congruent with our success- oriented beliefs through our consistent ethical convictions, words, and actions, individually and collectively.

There is a technique called the *as if* technique. It requires that we have a goal, and that we then do all we can to live *as if* that goal has already been actualized. For example, if our goal is to become more loving and we employ the *as if* technique, we begin to consider and feel ourselves to already be loving people. We begin to act *as if* we are loving, kind and compassionate, even if we may not actually feel those qualities in every situation or circumstance. We think of ourselves as already possessing the skills to love in universal and personal ways, and we act *as if* we are already skillful in these areas. Amazingly, with some hit and miss, our perceptions and attitudes begin to change and we lean more into the modes and the roles we seek to develop for ourselves, our children, families, schools, communities, and our world-at-large.

> I have learned this at least by my experiment: that as one advances confidently in the direction of his dreams, and endeavors to live the life which he has imagined, he will meet with a success unexpected in common hours. He will put some things behind, will pass an invisible boundary; new

universal...laws will begin to establish themselves around and within him; or the old laws will be expanded, and interpreted in his favor.

– Henry David Thoreau

Our success in demonstrating that a certain quality that we feel is valuable grows with practice and over some time. Again, what really counts first is our motivation and intention to serve our children and others around us for the purpose of upgrading all of our lives in the process. We can be assured that our efforts will bear positive if not perfect fruits. All the rest will follow.

> Ethical values are formulas of health, happiness, joy and bliss. These values are the spaceships taking you into Infinity and leaving behind the world of chaos and destruction. Be a value for the world.
>
> – Torkom Saraydarian
> *The Psyche and Psychism*, p. 894

References and Bibliography

Agni Yoga Society. New York: Agni Yoga Society.
Agni Yoga, 1980
Leaves of Morya's Garden, Vols. I and II, 1991 Brotherhood, 1962
New Era Community
American College Dictionary. New York: Random House, 1968
Anonymous Sedona, AZ: Aquarian Educational Group The Serene Life
Bailey, Alice A. New York: Lucis Publishing Co.
General quotations used from these writings.
Elkins, Dov Peretz
Glad to Be Me
Fromm, Erich
The Art of Loving
Gordon, Thomas
Parent Effectiveness Training (P.E.T.)
Gibran, Kahlil
The Prophet
Keyes, Ken
General writings
Montessori, Maria
Secret of Childhood and other writings
Saraydarian, Torkom. Sedona, AZ: Aquarian Educational Group. Challenge for Discipleship, 1986 (First printing) Christ, the Avatar of Sacrificial Love, 1974 (H. Saraydarian) The Flame of Beauty, Culture, Love, Joy, 1980
The Legend of Shamballa, 1976
The Psyche and Psychism, 1981

The Spring of Prosperity, 1982
Challenge for Discipleship, 1994 {Second printing)
The Heart and its Twelve Petals (Cave Creek, AZ: T.S.G. Publishing Foundation)
Shaw, George Bernard Man and Superman
Teilhard de Chardin, Pierre Omega Point

www.ingramcontent.com/pod-product-compliance
Lightning Source LLC
LaVergne TN
LVHW012249070526
838201LV00092B/166